Maybe once in a generation somebody is prepared to consecrate their entire life to the Lord. When it happens, God's true power is revealed to the world, as the lives of D.L.Moody, Billy Graham and Corrie ten Boom demonstrate. But John Lywood was an unlikely candidate for any list of good and faithful servants, beginning his life amidst unimaginable wealth and privilege, and blind to the very existence of God. But as he drove down Seven Mile Lane near West Malling in 1953, everything was about to change. This is John's story.

Also by Helen Wilkinson;

Dying to Live
The Missing Peace
Peter's Daughter
Chinks

Apostle to the Gypsies

The life story of Pastor John Lywood

by

Helen Wilkinson

stickleback books

APOSTLE TO THE GYPSIES

A STICKLEBACK BOOK

Published in England 2005 by Stickleback Books
an imprint of Ichthus Ltd
10 Park Plaza
Battlefield Industrial Estate
Shrewsbury, SY1 3AF

ISBN 0-9543105-3-5

Printed and bound in Great Britain by Biddles Ltd
Cover photograph © Courier Newspapers Tunbridge Wells
Cover design by River Media

www.sticklebackbooks.com
Email:sales@sticklebackbooks.com

For John,
because you loved the Lord.

And for all those who will read this story,
and believe.

Foreword by Jen Rees-Larcombe

Back in the 1970s, I had a remarkable experience in a Lent Discussion Group. We were a motley collection from various churches in the village; an Anglican Doctor, several boisterous Charismatics, an elderly strict Baptist and Brother Tom - a Roman Catholic monk, the monastery cook whose girth resembled Friar Tuck's.

One week he was full of a dream he'd had the previous night, 'Our Lord Himself came into my kitchen,' he told us breathlessly, 'So I cooked him a splendid meal - fish in a perfect cheese sauce, mashed potatoes and fresh green peas - but I woke up before I could see if He liked it!' Brother Tom looked as if he was going to cry with disappointment. But the following week he could not restrain the tears as he told us how a tramp had come to the kitchen door just as he was serving lunch to the Brothers. 'I had nothing left for him except my own plate of food,' said Brother Tom, 'So, very grudgingly, I slapped it down in front of him on the kitchen table. Then I suddenly realised the meal was fish in cheese sauce with fluffy white potatoes and new green peas. I couldn't stop weeping as I watched him enjoy every bite.'

The name of the tramp was Bill and when he finally finished his meal, he told Brother Tom about an extraordinary person he had recently met, 'Talks about God as if he knew him. I've been on the road for years, but I never met anyone like him before.

'I was on my way through Goudhurst last Sunday when I heard singing coming out of the village hall on the green, this little chap comes running out to say there was free grub going begging.   Little chap he is, old coat, shabby trilby, but sounds like a pure gent, born and bred.'

'Oh yes,' Brother Tom replied, 'That would be Pastor Lywood, everyone in Kent knows him! He's influenced me more than any other living man!'

'The hall was full of travellers, dossers, pickers and gentlemen of the road, but he got up and told us God loved us, all of us – even me - and I didn't get the name 'Burglar Bill' for nothing I can tell you! I'll be back there next Sunday for sure!'

It was more than another free lunch that had attracted Bill, and before long he had made a commitment to the Lord that lasted for the rest of his life. He was just one of thousands of men and women whose lives were changed by the little man in the shabby trilby who had once been a carefree rich kid, with the world at his feet. After a dramatic encounter with God, Pastor Lywood realised - like the rich young man in the gospels - that Jesus wanted him to sell everything he possessed and spend his life caring for the poor.

Years later he said, 'I was deeply touched by a verse in Matthew's Gospel which I read over and over again, focussing on the phrase, *'In as much as you have done it unto one of these the least of my brethren, you have done it unto me.'*

One day, when I visited his ramshackle congregation on Goudhurst village green, and sat listening to the stories of men and women from all over Kent and Sussex whom the 'Pastor' had led to the LORD and rescued from addiction, I said to him, 'When are you going to write a book about all this?'

'Never!' he replied, 'Too many of them need help to waste time writing about it!'

'But you bless so many of us with your brand of radical Christianity,' I told him, and I've kept on nagging ever since. Reading this riveting book at last has been a deeply moving experience for me. You may find your hair standing on end in the face of such outrageous faith, but I guarantee you will not be bored!

If I had not personally met many of the characters he mentions, I might well have found some of it hard to believe, but when you have watched rank 'No hopers' change into men and women whose confidence and dignity have been restored, you have no choice but to believe.

Pastor Lywood never hit the headlines, spoke on TV or travelled the world talking about his work. This book, that has been so difficult to persuade him to write, only tells a fraction of his story. Here on earth, the kind of down-and-outs he reached are considered by most of us to be worthless of notice, but one day, when we arrive in heaven, we will appreciate at last just what a major work of grace has been done in the last fifty years since that playboy met Jesus in Seven Mile Lane.

Jen Rees-Larcombe
August 2005

Many will see and put their trust in the Lord

A little old man, bent double by age, shuffles across the dining room at Cornford House towards me. He looks no different from any frail victim of Parkinson's disease in any nursing home in England. Struggling to make his body sit, he nods politely to the other residents at his table, then bends his head and gives thanks before eating.

Self-effacing, softly spoken, frail. Those are the words that come to mind as I sit opposite Charles John Lywood, the man who gave up everything for God.

* * *

It's September 2000 and the cashier at the filling station has just met another crackpot. A frail old man is paying for a tank of fuel for a battered white minibus. As he hands over the notes, he says to the cashier, 'The Lord has just told me to fill up our church minibus. He just said, 'Pull in and fill up with fuel.'

As he leaves, the old man smiles and says softly, 'God bless you,' to the cashier.

Three days later, the nation is in the grip of a fuel shortage, people can't get to work, there's no food in the supermarket and buses have stopped running. The cashier locks up the filling station now the last pump is empty, while a queue of vehicles snakes down the highway for almost a mile, hoping for a miraculous fuel delivery. On his long walk home, the cashier sees a battered white minibus dropping off a disabled woman and pulling away towards Goudhurst. Suddenly he remembers the words of the little old man one week ago.

* * *

I first met Pastor Lywood in 2000, after I'd heard about him from Jen Rees-Larcombe; 'He lived the life of a fabulously wealthy, jet-setting playboy. In his thirties he had a remarkable conversion experience,' she wrote intriguingly. 'He took seriously Jesus' command to sell all he had and give it to the poor. He's developed a remarkable work over the years among the down and outs, homeless, gypsies and Kentish hop-pickers, and he's seen some quite incredible miracles of healing. He has a wonderful story to tell.'

On my first visit, I expected to find someone who looked like a tramp, but spoke like an angel, an elderly new-age traveller. Something like that.

But Pastor Lywood is a Gentleman. With a capital 'G'.

'God bless you Helen,' he said softly, pronouncing my name He-*LIN*, 'So lovely to meet you. Lovely.'

Even shorter than my height of five feet two, wearing a collar and tie, he raised his twinkling dark eyes to mine, 'And you had a good journey of course, because I prayed for it.'

I had, yes, although that couldn't be connected with the frail little man standing in front of me. How could it?

A very large pinch of salt. That was what I'd decided in advance would be needed to make John's story palatable. I anticipated evangelism of the hell-fire-and-damnation variety, a compelling personality diverted from wealth and ambition years ago into religious mania.

But the man sitting opposite me wasn't manic. Evangelistic even. Just gentle, quiet and self-effacing.

I opened my notebook, smoothed the page. Thanked him for seeing me. Prepared to ask my first question.

But John had other ideas, 'Billy Graham once said, 'In certain circumstances, the worker is more important than the work.'

He leaned towards me intently, 'I think this is so in your case. I feel sure it is God's will for you to write this book, but in His strength, not your own. Whatever you do, don't write the book for me, write it for the Lord.'

12

I gulped.

So this is John's story, just as he told it to me, un-embellished. Corroborated by many hundreds of others, recorded by journalists, and set down now for a new generation.

When he began to tell me his story I was struck by two things, first John's Etonian accent, and second, his perfect recall. Unlike most people, he doesn't pause, clarify, or correct himself as he speaks - his words come assuredly, as though he's reading from a script.

He began, 'I think that if my story is written down in a book, it will help and encourage others. The Lord did give me a verse a little time ago when I was praying about this book. He said 'He being dead, yet speaketh.' [1] That's when I realised that after the Lord has called me home, He will still be speaking to others through my story.'

'Wow!' I said, trying to appear suitably impressed, but feeling dubious.

John saw through me immediately, 'Helin, do you believe and trust in the Lord Jesus Christ as your personal Saviour?'

'Well yes,' I answered, truthfully as it happens, because I had a life-changing conversion experience in 1994. But the world kind of gets in the way.... hey, you know how it is. Somehow I knew this wouldn't be the right thing to say out loud.

John was leaning forward intently, 'Because that's more important than anything Helin, that you believe and trust in Him.'

'Yes, I do,' I said, the flippancy fading, and beginning to doubt that I was the right one for this task. Mightn't there be some very holy and devout writer out there who could do this thing properly?

He settled back, and looked into space.

He was remembering. Taking himself back more than eighty years.

All things work together for the good of them that love God

I was born Charles John Lywood on 16 August 1923, a poor little rich boy into a family who had everything money could buy. My grandfather was a racehorse trainer, and my father was a qualified solicitor and Managing Director of a brewery firm. I was brought up as John and given an expensive private education, beginning at prep school in Swanage, then public school in Sherborne, Dorset.

I had everything I wanted, except the one thing I needed, and that was love. My dear mother was wonderful, but she never kissed or cuddled me, or put her arm round me once in the course of her whole life. I never saw my parents kiss, even once, because in our class in those days, families just didn't. When the young Prince Charles was separated from his mother for a long period in childhood they just shook hands when they were re-united. That really struck a chord with me when I saw it on the television news. We were like that.

So I was emotionally wounded before I began, and it would be another thirty years before I experienced any love.

War broke out in 1939 when I was 16 years old, and as soon as conflict was declared, I decided I wanted to fly. So the minute I was old enough, I volunteered for the RAF and began to train as a pilot.

By the time I signed up, new pilots had to be ready to fly solo after only eight hours of training. Pilot losses were drastic, and so few were coming back from missions that there wasn't enough time to train new recruits. So if you couldn't go solo in eight hours, you couldn't fly, and I never made it. If they'd given me another couple of hours

I think I would have done it. But they didn't.

I have an important confession to make from the very start. Years later, when I was recounting stories from my time in the RAF, some people had the impression that I'd been a pilot, and I never corrected them. When they said, 'Cor John, so you were a pilot in the war!' I just said, 'Yes.' And that wasn't true. I'm afraid that when they read this part of my story, they'll think I lied to them. That fear almost made me give up the idea of doing a book. I never meant to lie about this, and I've confessed it to the Lord, but I want to explain the truth now. Every word I'm going to tell you is true.

Because time ran out for me to become a pilot, I was appointed as Bomb Aimer in 199 squadron, and between 1943 and 1945, I ran 49 raids over Germany. Our plane was hit nearly every time we did a raid, and yet I was never shot down. The average number of raids carried out per person was only eight, so the chances of surviving 49 raids are absolutely amazing.

The Commanding Officer of squadron 199 said to my crew, 'You know the score, we're expecting you to do 30 raids. No-one's ever done it yet, but that's your job.'

We knew we were risking certain death or capture.

Our aircraft was almost always hit, but we never seemed to get hurt. On one occasion there were two German battleships waiting in Lorient harbour and Churchill gave the order for them to be destroyed, so the Allies went through in Midget submarines. But the Germans had put down nets, so our subs couldn't get through. Churchill decided the only way to destroy the battleships was by dropping mines from aircraft. Of course the harbour was very heavily defended.

To this day I don't know why they picked our crew to do it, maybe because we had such a high success rate. We had to wait for a clear, moonlit night and flew all the way to Lorient harbour from the south coast of England at treetop height to avoid the German radar. There were five of us aboard.

When we reached the harbour, we had to climb to 500 feet and drop the mines. As we climbed, I waited for the perfect moment and pressed the button.

I watched our mines go down, but was amazed to see a parachute appear - and the next minute they had us. Every searchlight was trained on us, and a hundred anti-aircraft guns riddled us with bullets, hitting our petrol tanks, all the way down our flank, the under-carriage, even our intercom was gone.

I knew what the Germans would do next - send up a fighter to finish us off. We didn't have long to wait, because sure enough, their fighter plane came from below and raked us from nose to tail a total of eight times.

But he just couldn't shoot us down. Even though we were already riddled with holes, he could not shoot us out of the sky.

Then the firing stopped - the German plane had obviously ran out of ammunition - because after the eighth attempt, he flew alongside us, (he was as near to us as that door is to me now), he saluted us, waggled his wings to us in a victory sign, and flew off. We knew he was indicating, '*You win!*'

All our petrol tank gauges were reading nought, and we kept flying, but our aircraft was dropping down and down and down.

I looked below, saw we were above a very rough sea and thought, 'We're going to ditch into that, and it isn't going to be pleasant.'

We hadn't any idea where we were, and just kept flying as long as we could in the direction we hoped was Britain.

Suddenly we saw land ahead, and assumed it was

Ireland. We thought we'd bypassed England altogether. But as I looked down, and this sounds almost unbelievable - but in the name of Jesus it's exactly what happened - I recognised my parents' large white house on the Ex estuary, directly below us.

I shouted to the pilot, 'We're in Exmouth'. I knew the whole estuary. Fortunately, although our intercom wasn't working, our mayday signal was OK, and we just signalled, 'Mayday, mayday, mayday.' They shot searchlights up to us from Exeter airport which was only eight miles away. I knew the terrain like the back of my hand and was able to guide us in. We prepared for a crash landing, but I still thought we were done for. I said to myself, 'This plane is soaked with petrol, so when we crash land, the whole lot's going up.'

We thundered down, waited, but there was no explosion. Not a single one of the crew of five was hurt, except the Rear Gunner who had a minor leg injury.

When the plane was inspected it was a piece of wreckage, and looked like something on a dump yard. I couldn't understand it, nobody could, not one of the engineering staff on the base could explain how we had stayed airborne, never mind reached home.

Night after night this unbelievable experience went round and round in my head. I just couldn't forget it. Although I wasn't a Christian, didn't pray and certainly didn't believe in God, I used to lie in bed and think - how is it that all my friends are dead, everybody I know has been shot down, and I'm still alive? Why? How can this have happened?

I just could *not* believe what had happened to us, and never talked to anybody about it, not even to the rest of the crew. It wasn't until ten years later, about three or four months after I'd been converted that I realised - That's why! God kept me alive for a reason!

After our first 15 raids, they put us on Stirlings which were death traps because they couldn't fly above 20,000 feet and the RAF was finding they wouldn't fly successfully even at this height, so our squadron inherited the whole fleet. The entire squadron were put on Stirlings for about six weeks except our crew. After our desperate raid on Lorient harbour, the Commanding Officer took us off duty and sent us on holiday. So I avoided the Stirlings more than most, and that probably saved my life again.

Our pilot, a Geoffrey Archer, was a great favourite of mine, and he was a truly brilliant pilot. On one mission, we took off in a Stirling at about midnight to bomb Milan in Italy, and our route lay over the Alps.

As we took off, I was shocked when Geoffrey swung us off the runway. Instead of turning back and having another go as he should have done, Geoffrey pulled the throttle right back and I saw we were taking off obliquely, I just couldn't imagine what he was thinking of. This was completely out of character for a man who never made a mistake.

Suddenly in front of me I saw a great wall, and thought - this is it. This time I'm dead. We shot vertically up the wall and away, and as we shot up, there was an almighty crash and bang, but somehow we were still airborne.

Ground control never broke radio silence in England, because the Germans could pick it up, but for the first time ever they broke the code and called to us, 'Are you all right?'

We replied, 'We're all right'. That was all.

We didn't know it at the time, but when we returned from the mission we found we had just clipped the wall of a bomb dump. Any closer and we would have been matchwood.

Our Stirling couldn't fly high enough to cross the summit of Mont Blanc, so we knew we would have to fly to the side of the mountain, rather than over the top.

But just before we reached the Alps, one of our four engines packed up as a result of the earlier impact, so we only had three working engines. We could now only fly at a maximum of 10,000 feet.

As we approached the mountains, the pilot said to us, 'What do you think boys?'

I said, 'We'd better turn back – because we'll never get through the Alps flying at this height.'

But the Rear Gunner chipped in, 'Why don't we have a go?'

So we all agreed to try it.

I'll never forget that moment. It was a brilliant, clear night with the moon shining on the snow-capped Alps, the scene below was breathtaking. We had to fly up and down, hugging the mountain-side, cutting through the ravines, and trying not to crash our plane straight into the walls of every chasm.

Against all the odds, we got through, dropped our bombs on Milan and set off again for home.

We all agreed we couldn't attempt to use the same route back through the Alps, it would be madness, and decided to fly to allied territory in North Africa, and land there.

But the navigator did some calculations and said, 'We can't do it. We just haven't got enough fuel,' so we had no choice. Geoffrey headed back to the Alps and took us through, repeating the desperate flight through moonlit ravines.

When we landed, he was awarded an immediate DFC - the very next morning he had to go to Buckingham Palace to receive it. I always felt that was ironic, because the whole incident was caused by his poor flying in the first place.

But we were preserved, that was the extraordinary thing. I never recognised the true significance until after I got converted. It was utterly miraculous.

A few nights ago I saw a programme called *The Battlefields of Yesterday* on BBC2. They showed bombing raids like ours, and the pictures took me right back sixty years. Suddenly it hit me again, how miraculous it was that the Lord preserved me. I had done 49 successful raids, where most crews did only five or six. A total of 30 raids was known as a Tour, and nobody but us ever achieved a Tour in our squadron. It was such a miracle, and after watching the programme, I thanked and praised God again and again. The TV pictures brought it all back, I could almost feel the bullets going in one side of our plane and out the other and never hitting me. Things impossible to explain. It was divine protection, and although I didn't thank Him then, I thank the Lord now.

Recently I saw Speilberg's *Band of Brothers*, and in one scene a young lieutenant said, 'How can I cope with all this bloodshed?'

The reply came back, 'Be absolutely sure you're going to die, and then you'll be able to carry out your duty without compassion.'

With the force of a blow I realised - That's exactly what I have done, I did that! Before every single raid I thought – 'I know I'm not going to live,' so I felt hardly any fear at all, just assumed I was going to die.

When I heard those words on the film, they struck to my heart, I'd never heard anybody else echoing my sentiment before. But that's how I lived through the war, and how I managed to climb into the plane every single time.

Years later I met two other people who had similar experiences of God's miraculous protection. On a train in the rush hour when all the carriages were full, I noticed the seat opposite me was empty, even though people were standing in the corridors. I guessed the Lord was keeping the seat empty for a special reason. The carriage got more crowded, the whistle blew, and the train pulled out of Charing Cross. Then a man came rushing up the carriage and sat in the seat saying, 'That was a close shave! I didn't think I was going to catch it.'

I noticed a fish on the lapel of his suit jacket.

'Praise the Lord!' I said to him.

'Oh praise the Lord.'

'Do you know - God kept that seat free so we could meet.'

We started talking. He had been a missionary in India with his wife and told me a remarkable story, 'There have been riots in Calcutta and they've been killing whites - especially Christians. A few weeks ago my wife and I were abducted by a gang who separated us, lined me up against a wall and ordered seven soldiers to shoot me. Their rifles went up, another order was given, and I heard the safety catches click. I knew that in the next second, seven bullets would plunge into my brain. But I'd never felt such perfect peace as I felt at that moment, it was God's perfect peace. The bullets never came. My wife and I were both spared.'

Later, I met a minister in London who told me how during the war his submarine was charged by a German battleship and water started pouring in. They knew they would drown, everyone was shouting and screaming. He said exactly what the other man had, that he'd never felt such perfect peace in all his life as at that moment. He and one other man from the entire crew were saved.

Blessed are the pure in heart,
for they shall see God

When the war ended, I was the most surprised person in the world, and remember thinking, 'What on earth am I going to do now? I was supposed to be dead!' It was very difficult to re-adjust to the idea of living, and I don't think I ever did adjust until I got converted ten years later.

You see that photo on my wall? I don't know why I kept it, but sub-consciously it must have been for the same reason, to remind me of the miracle of my survival. It's me when I was 22, wearing the DFC – the Distinguished Flying Cross.

The next part of my story is difficult to tell, and I don't want to hurt any members of my family by it. By 1944 I was twenty-one years old, but had absolutely no idea that my father had left his wife before moving in with my mother. His wife and her family were all deeply religious, and in those days people were shunned if they divorced, so my parents had fled to Devon where they lived together and I grew up.

The scandal was kept quiet and because there hadn't been a divorce, my parents weren't able to marry. I was completely unaware that I had an entire family of cousins and grandparents, as well as a half-brother and half-sister; my father's first two children. The whole situation was kept hush-hush.

When I was awarded the DFC, I was pictured in the local paper, with the caption, *John Lywood, the only son of Mr and Mrs Charles Lywood.* Somehow my father's wife saw the picture, and soon afterwards my father had legal notification that she intended to bring a case to court to prove that I was not his only son.

So the truth was about to become public, and my

mother had to sit me down and tell everything - that my parents weren't married, and that I had a half-brother and sister. It was so hard for her to do.

Only five years ago I discovered another half-brother whose existence was unknown to me for seventy-five years.

My father didn't live long after this, and it was a very difficult time in our family.

I do believe the Lord can speak to people at the time of their death, perhaps even after we would consider them to be medically dead. And I'm certain that happened to my father. He had never given any indication whatsoever that he had a faith, never talked about God, and never went to church except on rare special occasions.

One day just after the war was over, as I walked into the house my mother announced, 'Your father is dead.'

I stopped in my tracks.

'Do you want to go and see him?' she asked.

I walked into the bedroom and was shocked by the sight that met my eyes. All the lines had gone out of my father's face and he looked about my own age, early twenties. And he had an expression in his eyes as though he'd seen something utterly wonderful. I call that expression 'Surprised by joy.' I knew he'd seen something marvellous, but had absolutely no idea what it could be.

Ten years later, after my own conversion, I was going through some old cuttings and found the leaflet from the funeral reception of my father's father, Mr Edwin Lywood. I only knew that he was a well-known expert on plants, but we had never met.

The leaflet read, 'Mr Edwin Lywood became converted in his middle life and became a Methodist preacher.'

As I read this, I felt absolutely certain that he must have been the one who prayed for my father, and prayed for me. There's always somebody praying for you, our lives are beautifully connected. The Lord will reveal it if you ask Him.

After my conversion I did just that, and this is what I found out.

All the time that I'd been in the RAF I was pretty wild, drinking and partying heavily. I really did burn the candle at both ends, and didn't value my life.

During the evacuation my mother had written to me saying, 'When you come home on leave you're going to find a surprise – there are two girls staying with us.'

My parents' home was beautiful, and my mother wrote that when the evacuation assessors had visited my father, he'd told them, 'Sorry, I'm not having a lot of snotty-nosed little children running round my lovely house.'

We had a marine camp nearby, and my father heard that if you offered rooms to a couple of W.R.E.N.s, you could avoid being forced to have evacuated children.

So he rang the Commanding Officer and offered to take two W.R.E.N.s.

One was a farmer's daughter called Honour, she talked away like anything, and the other was a tiny mouse-like girl from Scotland who never wore lipstick, never smoked and hardly spoke.

When I came home on leave, eager to meet these two young women, I found the little Scottish girl was terrified of me. Honour said to my mother one day, 'I don't know what that girl does, when I go to sleep she's on her knees praying, and when I wake up she's still on her knees praying.'

The Lord told me after I got converted that she'd been the one praying for me. I tried to find her, but my mother and Honour had lost contact with her. I owe her a debt of gratitude.

During the war there were hunts all over England,

and one of the most famous was the Quorn hunt where the Prince of Wales had stayed before the war. It was at a Quorn hunt that I first met the girl who would become my wife. Her background was very similar to mine, and her father was a wealthy landowner. We seemed to have plenty in common.

My squadron were stationed right in the middle of the land used by the hunt, and on one occasion a horse dealer got hold of me and said, 'You're a very good rider, would you like to ride some of my horses and help me sell them?'

'I certainly would,' I replied, and after this I had thousands of pounds worth of hunting absolutely free. Through the hunt I met Sir George Earl who was Managing Director of Portland Cement and we became firm friends.

When the war came to an end, I decided to leave the RAF. Although I was a flight lieutenant, and could have stayed on, I needed to earn enough money to support the lifestyle I'd come to expect and enjoy, both as a child and since.

Because of the war I'd missed out on university and had no training in anything, and decided to go into the brewing business where I knew I could earn a very good living. The only thing that motivated me in those days was making money.

So I went into my father's company and spent all my spare time hunting, racing and playing every kind of sport. I'd always been a great sportsman, excelling at golf, tennis, squash, all of that, but especially riding.

Money was flowing, I had a very good job, and then my father died.

Around this time, for some inexplicable reason, I became troubled by a certain knowledge that when I reached thirty, something dramatic was going to happen to me. I never thought of God, just knew something momentous was going to happen - but didn't have a clue what.

After my father's death, and with this premonition of the future, I had a terrific urge to get to London and learn everything I could in business as fast as possible. So I contacted my friend Sir George Earl and asked him to take me into his business at Portland Cement.

He didn't have a place, but recommended his friend Colonel Bill Whitbread who owned a hugely successful brewery. Sir George wrote to Bill and asked him to take me on. Soon I heard from Bill who asked me to run his two hundred Kent pubs.

So that's what brought me to Kent. For the next five years I ran those pubs and became really wealthy. Bill made me Director of Lenys Brewery at Wateringbury and I had more money than I could spend. I had race horses, new cars every year, and a very good salary.

After I moved to Kent, my widowed mother sold the family home in Exmouth and bought a house in Tunbridge Wells so she could be close to me.

By the winter of 1953 I was thirty, happily married, and the youngest Director in the firm.

What happened to me next was so holy and amazing that I've told very few people about it in the course of my whole life. Jesus said, *'Cast not your pearls before swine nor give what is holy to the dogs,'* [2] so I've always been very careful who I've told.

At a later stage John and I had a discussion about the rights and wrongs of putting the next part of his testimony into this book. John was worried for two reasons, that some people may not believe it was true, or that it would be wrong to describe something so holy. It was my opinion, then and now, that the incident on a winter afternoon in 1953 was so important that it couldn't be left out.

While John described the next scene to me, his demeanour changed. He leaned forward, spoke softly, and looked even holier, if that were possible.

One evening, soon after my thirtieth birthday in 1953, I was driving back to my office at the brewery after a day spent driving around some of my pubs. It's important to tell you that I *never* drank on duty. Never, ever. It wouldn't be true to say I never had a drink in the evenings, but I never once drank when I was visiting the pubs. My usual routine was to visit seven or eight of my pubs a day, then return to the office.

On this occasion, I'd finished at the last pub and was on the Seven Mile Lane just outside West Malling. It was about four o'clock in the evening, and the sky was just getting dark.

Suddenly, without a hint of warning, the sky in front of me opened and I had a sight of heaven. An open sight of it. It wasn't a vision, but a sighting of something real.

I saw Jesus sitting on the great white throne and the angels around Him singing. It was absolutely, indescribably beautiful. I clearly saw the angels and saw Jesus, and then He spoke to me, and His voice was like the voice of many waters, and this is what he said, '*Blessed are the pure in heart.*'

Then the sky closed and I carried on driving. This had just happened to a man who didn't even believe in God, never mind in Jesus.

My heart turned over in my chest and I was filled with such wonder, awe, amazement, disbelief, love and joy - all at once. It was as real as you are, and I was still driving along when the sky closed, and suddenly I noticed a telephone box. I pulled over, stopped the car, and phoned my secretary at the brewery to say, 'I won't be in today after all, I'll be in tomorrow.'

Then I got back into my car, still full of turbulent emotions - disbelief, wonder and love.

The exact spot on Seven Mile Lane where it happened is a holy place to me, and every time I've driven down there since, I recall the same thing, and whenever I'm praising the Lord, that's the picture I see in my mind.

There are other people who've had an open sight of heaven, although I may be the only one alive now. It happened to Smith-Wigglesworth, the great Pentecostal preacher, who saw the same sight, not a vision, but a sighting through a miraculous opening of the sky.

I didn't know what to do, and without understanding why, drove straight into Tunbridge Wells to buy a Bible. That's what I did, drove straight there, walked into the bookshop and said, 'I want a Bible.'

The bookseller said, 'What sort of a Bible would that be sir?'

'I don't know, any Bible, I just want a Bible'. I had never owned one.

Of course money was no object, and when the bookseller said, 'This is a very, very good one sir, and has a concordance,' I offered to buy it immediately because it was expensive. I didn't even know what a concordance was.

So I paid for the precious Bible, an authorised King James version, and took it straight home. I knew I was holding something of great value, although I didn't understand how or why. Strangely enough, I didn't say a word to my wife, just took the Bible upstairs.

The words I'd heard Jesus speak were still ringing in my ears, *'Blessed are the pure in heart,'* and I hoped to find them somewhere in this Bible. But I didn't know where to look, whether they would be in the Old Testament or the New, or how to begin searching.

I sat down and turned to the back of the book, and immediately understood what a concordance was - an index of the words and phrases to be found in the Bible itself. The concordance enabled me to look up the phrase I had just heard from heaven. The reference was Matthew chapter 5 verse 8, and I leafed through to find the place. When my eyes fell on the verse I was amazed, because the words were written exactly as Jesus had spoken them to me, '*Blessed are the pure in heart,*' and they were followed by the promise, '*for they shall see God.*'

'Well that's exactly what I've done!' I thought, 'I've had an open sight of Heaven and I've seen God!'

I sat looking at the text for a long time, pondering on the words.

But my experience, and new realisation that God must exist, didn't mean that I was converted, saved or forgiven. I had no understanding of salvation, or any idea of what Jesus had done for me on the cross. I didn't know anything at all. The more I thought about my sighting of Jesus, the more concerned I became that no-one would believe me if I told them, so I decided to keep silent about the whole event. The moment on Seven Mile Lane was so powerful and holy to me, that I didn't dare share it with another soul, for fear of being doubted or challenged. My silence even extended to my wife.

From the moment I had that sight of Jesus, I began to experience the love I'd never had in childhood or since.

The initial effect on me was a decision to try and live a better life, a Godly life very different from my past, although at that stage I had no idea how dramatically the event would alter the course of my whole future. I just planned to read the Bible now and again, and perhaps go to church.

Although I'd said nothing, my wife must have noticed a change in me because after a couple of days she said,

'John, you've changed, you're different.'
    'How do you mean different?' I asked her.
    'I don't know, just different somehow.'
    And still I said nothing.

Follow thou Me

Before that winter afternoon I never attended church or went near any Christian people. But the conviction began to grow inside me that I must start to attend church regularly. I was familiar with the old C of E prayer book from public school chapel, and even though I'd been taught to repeat some collects and the creed, the words hadn't meant a thing to me.

I needed to talk to someone who may be able to help me understand what I'd seen, and after a while I decided to call on our local Anglican vicar. All I knew about vicars was they were Godly people who had white collars round their necks, and might be able to tell me what to do next.

So I described the sighting, simply and honestly, exactly as it had happened.

I could tell right away he didn't believe me.

'Are you married?' he asked.

'Yes.'

'Any children?'

'Yes, two young ones.'

'Hmm. Maybe God is speaking to you in this vision and calling you to be a clergyman, I'll get in touch with the Bishop of Rochester and see what he thinks.'

Not long afterwards I had an invitation to lunch with the Bishop and we chatted during the meal. This time I'd decided not to speak of my sight of heaven, fearing he wouldn't believe me.

The Bishop said, 'I can see you're a good man and you want to follow God. I'm quite impressed with you, and it's clear you've also got sound business experience. I tell you what - if you agree to take a theological course at Wycliffe College in Oxford for twelve months, then I'll give you a parish.'

'Thank you very much,' I replied, trusting that a Bishop must know best.

I returned home and started to read the Bible and Book of Common Prayer in earnest, knowing that if I was to become a clergyman, I must believe the words I'd be required to say in services. But the more I read, the more uncomfortable I became.

I thought, 'When I'm christening a baby, the parents may be un-believers, and I'll be legally obliged to baptise their child. After I sprinkle water over the baby and hand it back to the parents I'll have to say, *'See now Dearly Beloved, this child is now regenerate.'* And that's not right!' I said to myself as I read.

Hunting through my new Bible, I tried to corroborate the words of the baptism service with God's word, and they didn't match. I couldn't find anything about babies being baptised and being regenerate.

My uncertainty grew, and although I had been accepted to study at Oxford, two days before I was due to go up, I withdrew from my place. I heard that the Bishop of Rochester was absolutely furious when he found out, and he never spoke to me again.

I had no idea what to do next, but had begun to pray to the God I'd seen, and felt certain He wanted me to give up my job at the Brewery.

So I resigned, and Colonel Whitbread was so angry that he too refused to speak to me again. It seemed my new faith was making me a lot of enemies. At first I had no financial worries - we had shares and investments to live on - and I simply waited to see where my faith would lead. My wife must have been very anxious during the two years that we lived in this way, with me out of work, doing very little, and saying even less to her about my situation.

All this time I was becoming closer and closer to the

Lord, and I spent a lot of time studying the Bible and attending church.

My initial thought about attending church after my conversion was, 'Now I must join the true church,' meaning the Roman Catholics. I knew Catholics say theirs is the true church, so I went straight to a service. Resolving not to speak to anyone in case they tried to persuade me, I decided to pick up their pamphlets and see for myself what they believe.

I took their literature home and quickly found that they contained contradictions to the Bible. For example, Catholics are encouraged to pray for the dead, which is not biblical. I could only find one Bible verse on that subject, which indicated that the early church used to baptise the son of a person who had died in his place.[3] But nothing at all about praying for souls of the dead.

So I thought, 'I've either got to believe the Bible or believe Rome.' I was in a quandary and knew that if I asked a Catholic priest, he would tell me to become a Catholic, and if I asked an Anglican, he'd say the opposite.

'So what's the use of asking men?' I thought.

And I did what I nearly always do, went down on my knees and asked the Lord which church I should attend. Immediately He revealed to me that the Bible is the truth.

First He led me to read the Book of Revelation about the Harlot of Babylon, and early the next morning, for a full two hours, the Lord poured into me the truth of His word.

Later in the day I walked down the road, and met a very godly clergyman I knew by repute, although we'd never spoken. I asked him about what the Lord had said, and he gave me the confirmation I needed.

Soon afterwards I went to collect some Christian tracts to hand out, and while I was waiting for them to be packed, I idly picked up a Plymouth Brethren book showing where catholic doctrine was false and the Bible was right.

So I had three separate confirmations of the truth of scripture.

For a while I attended our very traditional local Anglican church, but soon moved to an evangelical free church in Tunbridge Wells. Going to church and reading the Bible were enough to occupy me, and I wasn't worried about the future.

During this period of waiting, someone invited me to a Christian event aimed at people from the south-east who had been converted. I was told there would be other guests like me, including wealthy city stockbrokers.

I went along, and was making my way to the front when to my absolute horror, I spotted one of my old drinking pals, with his wife and children.

With a bolt to the heart I knew I should go right up to him in the middle of the meeting, and witness about my conversion. 'Oh no!' I thought, 'what on earth is he going to say when he hears I've been converted?'

So I couldn't find the courage to face him, and tried to blend into the background, hoping he wouldn't spot me. But after a while I knew I had to confront my fear, and went over to him gingerly.

'Hello John!' he beamed, 'How are you?'

I blurted out straight away, 'Hello! I've got something to tell you. Since we last met, I've been converted.'

'Well praise the Lord! So have I!' he replied, slapping me on the back. That was a wonderful moment as I felt the Lord showing me I needn't be fearful of owning Him.

It was hard to be obedient in those early days, when I still trailed so much of my former life behind me, with all it represented. But through incidents like this, I began to learn the truth of the verse, *'The Holy Spirit is given to them that obey.'* [4]

Perhaps I should explain that from the earliest days after my sight of heaven, I've had two ways of receiving God's guidance, neither of which were taught to me, I simply knew them to be right.

The first is to open my Bible while I pray, letting the pages fall open at random. Whenever I've needed direction I do this, and can honestly say that in the fifty years since coming to faith, every time God's words have always jumped off the page into my heart and understanding. Many years later, experienced Christians told me not to pray like this, but by then I'd done it so many times and God had already proved the truth of it. So I never felt the need to listen to their advice. This is a case of the saying, 'Good is very often the enemy of the best'. Sometimes people offer human sympathy to a person who really needs to trust the Lord themselves, and be told so. Very often, if you give out human sympathy at that time, you're giving the good instead of the best. What people need is the truth. Never forget Ananias and Sapphira who were punished for lying to God.[5]

The second way that God directs me, is by direct word. I've been asked whether I hear audible words, and I don't, but when the Lord guides me by direct command, I can always tell clearly what he wants me to do. His Spirit guides and shows me.

Very soon after my experience on Seven Mile Lane, I read in my Bible, *'Jesus is the way, the truth and the life.'*[6] These words played on my mind and I thought, 'But what about Moslems and Hindus and all the different faiths? They don't believe in Jesus, so what about them?

I asked various ministers around the area, and none of them gave me a proper answer that I could accept. At that time there was a vicar who everybody held in great esteem - John Stott, vicar of All Souls in Langham Place. A couple of months after my conversion, I went up to see him.

'It's very good of you to spare the time to see me,' I said, 'And I'd like you to answer a question. Jesus said He is the only way to God.'

'Yes.'

'Well what's going to happen to all the Moslems, Hindus and Sikhs?'

John Stott talked about this and that, and when I left him I was no wiser than when I'd arrived. He gave me completely unsatisfactory answers.

So I came home and thought, 'It's no good asking people, not one of them can give you the answer,' so I went down on my knees and said, 'Lord, please could you give me the answer?' Then I opened the Bible and read the words, *What's that to you? Follow thou me.*'[7] So in other words God was saying to me - mind your own business about the fate of other people, just follow me! That's my business not yours.

And that's a perfect answer.

One summer afternoon in 1956, more than two years after my conversion, I wandered into St John's Church in Tunbridge Wells, and found it completely empty and hushed. It's a big, holy building and I had a sudden overwhelming conviction of the need to have my sins forgiven.

I dropped to my knees and vowed that I wouldn't get up until I knew my sins had been forgiven. I spent two full hours praying and asking for my sins to be washed away.

In my pocket was a little edition of the New Testament, and after two hours I reached inside and pulled out the little book. Letting the pages fall open, immediately the verse jumped out at me, *Jesus Christ His own self took our sins in His own body upon the cross.*[8]

In a flash the Holy Spirit revealed the truth of that verse to me, and all at once I knew and understood that Jesus had paid the price for me and had taken all my sins away. I felt washed and cleansed - the burden of my sins had lifted from me.

I almost skipped out of the church into the afternoon sunshine and felt as though I was walking two feet above the pavement. I was completely and utterly cleansed.

Two days later it hit me, 'I've been born again,' I thought, 'that's what has happened to me. That's what it means!'

Immediately I got down on my knees, 'Whatever you want me to do Lord,' I prayed, 'I'll do it. Wherever you want me, I'll go. If you send me to Africa, Burma, or Timbuktu, I'll go. Please show me what you want me to do, and whatever it is, I'll do it.'

As I was praying, I opened the Bible and read these words, *'You are not called to a people of a hard language, or difficult speaking.'*[9]

'Well that rules out being a Missionary,' I thought, 'So He's got something else for me.'

During the first years of my ministry I was deeply touched by a verse in Matthew's Gospel which I read over and over again, focussing on the phrase, *'In as much as you have done it unto one of these the least of my brethren, you have done it unto me.'*[10]

In the whole of my past life I'd had absolutely no interest in anybody less wealthy than me, or of lower social status. I only mixed with the privileged classes and had no time for others, I was the life and soul of the party, and the only person I really cared about was myself.

But the verse in Matthew made me think about dossers, down and outs, and people forced to sleep rough. God had begun to change me and give me a great love for people.

My life is evidence that the Lord can change us, and I still see it happening today. A professional man I've met recently was once a brutal drunkard, and yet he's now one of the kindest and most thoughtful people I've ever met. The transformation in him and me is nothing short of miraculous. God does alter us through Christ.

One morning the Lord gave me a vision of a motley group of people, shuffling along in dirty, filthy clothes, and wearing hopeless faces. Immediately God filled me to the fullness with His love and compassion for these people. The power and intensity of the love that fell upon me was too much, and I couldn't take any more. I begged, 'Please stay your hand Lord, this feeling of love and tenderness is unbearable.'

Then God poured out his compassion for these down and outs, and laid it all on me. I thought, 'This has got to stop, or I'm going straight to heaven, I just can't take any more.'

I believe I then received a real understanding of God's response to the loveless in our world. He loves them so much, it's wonderful to see.

I was left with a tremendous urge to help and love people like those I'd seen in the vision, and during my early years of ministry I began a mission with dossers and down and outs. It became common knowledge that I was an unofficial pastor to these people.

They respond to love, and still come to visit me, I never know when they're coming, they just drop in for ministry or prayer, and to hear God's word.

During 1957 I frequently went up to London to seek out homeless people in the city. The Lord particularly encouraged me to work under Charing Cross Bridge, where many dossers bedded down. Late one summer night I was tired and had decided to catch a train home, but as I walked away, the Lord spoke to me powerfully, 'Stay a bit longer.' It was dark and late, and I longed to be tucked up in bed, but turned back.

As I passed a narrow dark alley, the Lord told me to go into it. I knew it was a crazy thing to do, but obeyed. As my eyes got used to the darkness, I saw about twenty piles of rubbish heaped in the alley. When I got closer, I noticed that the piles were actually sleeping men.

I prayed, 'I can't do anything about this Lord, they're all asleep.' So I began to pray for the men, on that lovely night.

While I prayed, one of the heaps moved, and a man roused himself, got up and staggered towards me. He was stocky, about fifty or fifty-five, and had an absolutely murderous face. He was a truly terrible sight as he lurched towards me.

'Good evening,' I said, and he made a sort of growling noise at me, I could smell the stench of drink on his breath.

'Can I get you a cup of tea or coffee?' I asked.

Then he raised his arm above my head, and I knew if I said another word, he would slam his fist into my face. I just knew he was going to hit me, so I closed my eyes and spoke to him, 'You can hit me if you like, but before you do, let me say this; God loves you, and Jesus died for you.'

And the blow never came. I paused, opened my eyes and saw the burly tramp standing next to me with tears pouring down his filthy cheeks. He grabbed my arm fiercely and begged, 'Pray for me, pray for me!'

So we stood together and I prayed aloud for the man. Then I had to leave, but he remained in my thoughts.

I went home and a week later a friend phoned.

'John,' he said, 'I've got a dosser off the road, taken him in and given him something to eat, but I can't get anywhere with him. He's a rough, aggressive one, but you know about these people. Would you come and help?'

'Yes of course,' I said and went straight to his house.

As I stepped inside I gasped, because here was the very same man I had prayed with in the alley only a week before.

In the next few days I learned the man's story, his name was Bobby Freer, and he had been brought up in the Gorbles in Glasgow before the war. Bobby had got involved with knife gangs who plagued the city, and at eighteen he joined the Merchant Navy to get passage to America. When they docked, he jumped ship and got mixed up with street gangs, fighting and robbing. It was the only life he knew.

During a robbery, one of the gang shot a victim dead, and the police arrested Bobby and the culprit, (who went to the electric chair). Bobby was sentenced to twenty years, and when he was released, he returned to England, became an alcoholic and lived rough. Now I understood why he had the murderous look in his eyes on the night we met.

Very soon after I met Bobby, he gave up drinking and started coming to church. He accepted the truth of the Gospel, and he was one of the very first people I had led to the Lord since my own salvation.

I carried on working with the down and outs and dossers rejected by society, but - thank the Lord - He has chosen the weak and sinners.

Friends used to ask me, 'How do you find all these people John?' But the truth was I didn't find them, the Lord sent them to me. And they kept on coming.

I continued to pray about men who are rejected by society, scorned by people like I'd once been, and as I was praying, the Lord gave me an understanding of a great truth, *'Those whom are despised hath God chosen.'*[11] Suddenly I understood – God very often calls the people nobody wants, and He blesses and uses them in mighty ways. Conversely, often the people the world loves are not the ones God calls.

This was never more true than in the case of Fred Scruton, a dosser I first met in Maidstone, hunched up in an oversized black overcoat, with long dark hair and a scruffy beard, and a shuffling way of walking. When I first saw him across the street it was night time, and I felt the Lord say to me, 'Go over and minister to that man.' It's always dangerous approaching these men at night, you never know if they'll react violently, but I trusted in the Lord and approached the hunched figure.

'Good evening,' I said.

To my surprise he answered politely, 'Good evening.'

The Lord told me, 'Pray for him.'

So I said, 'I'm going to pray for you dear friend,' and laid my hand on him and prayed aloud.

When I finished he had tears streaming down his face, just as Bobby Freer had done before him. He was saying, 'I felt him. I felt him!'

'Who?' I asked.

'Jesus, I felt Jesus.'

By God's grace I took Fred back to Tunbridge Wells with me and got him fitted up in new clothes. He looked an utterly different man. He was baptised later and followed the Lord with all his heart. Later he would become my companion as we travelled the roads together, and come with me to represent accused men in court.

On a cold, wet winter evening in Maidstone, after I'd been walking all day and preaching to the many dossers in the town, I had a little bit of money left for a bus fare home to Tunbridge Wells, with enough spare to buy someone a cup of tea and a sandwich. I saw a down-and-out, approached him, and offered him tea and a sandwich.

He said, 'That would be wonderful, I've had nothing

to eat all day.'

We found a café where I bought him tea, shook his hand, said 'God bless you,' and turned to leave. I had enough for my bus fare - the exact amount and no more. It was raining and cold outside.

But as I reached the door, I heard the Lord say, 'Go back and give him the money you've got in your pocket.'

'Oh no Lord, ' I begged, 'I'm so tired, how am I going to get home without the money?'

'Go back and give him all the money you've got in your pocket.'

So I walked back into the café and said, 'There you are my friend, that might help you later.'

He thanked me and I went out into the cold, wet night.

So there was only one thing to do, walk and trust God to get a lift, even though I was tired, hungry and thirsty. I walked to the outskirts of Maidstone praying all the time, until eventually a car stopped.

The driver said, 'I'm only going as far as Hadlow.'

'That's OK, I thank and praise the Lord for that.'

'Isn't the Lord wonderful?' he said.

He was a Christian. When we reached Hadlow he said, 'I tell you what, how about coming to have a nice meal with my family, and I'll run you home to Tunbridge after that?'

We had a lovely meal, a blessing I'd have missed if I'd caught the bus, and then he drove me home. By giving away the money, the Lord had blessed me greatly, and yet again proved how important it is to be obedient when he speaks. It is then He really acts.

God shall supply all your needs

During the early months after my conversion, I received another call from the Lord. I heard Him say, 'You're to give up everything and give away all your money. You have got to live by faith.'

When I heard these words, I was absolutely, completely terrified, and spent almost two years trying to ignore the instruction. I know now, as I didn't then, that God calls very few people to give away their money and live by faith. Some non-believers think all Christians are required to be poor, but this isn't true. Only in a few rare cases does God ask an individual to trust Him alone for earthly provision. The fact that I was once a privileged, spoiled young man may have been part of the reason that God called me to live by faith. I have a great deal of sympathy for the rich young ruler of the Gospel story who couldn't be parted from his money to follow Jesus. And a long, weary time passed before I gave in.

A pattern had emerged that I didn't share my faith with my wife as I should have done, so I told her nothing of this command, and worried about it, asking God, 'But what about my wife and beautiful children, if I live by faith they won't have enough to eat? Everything will go wrong Lord!'

I was consumed with fear, because living by faith was a concept I simply couldn't embrace. I knew nobody with any experience of living this way, and didn't understand or believe in it, although I knew deep down in my heart that this was God's unswerving call for me.

But I resisted every nudge, and closed my mind to the command that I must renounce all my wealth, live by faith, and trust Him for everything. I told myself that if I had no wife or children, I could have done it. And I knew I was doing wrong.

For two years I closed my ears, and then once again St John's Church in Tunbridge Wells proved to be the place where I found help. I'd gone there for a fete, during this phase of fighting God's will, and as I ambled from stall to stall, I spotted a little book on a table. It was called *'Retrospect'* by Hudson Taylor, a name that meant nothing to me, but I felt led by the Lord to buy it, paid sixpence and put the book in my pocket.

When I returned home and started to leaf through the book, I could hardly believe my eyes. The little volume was a handbook explaining how to live by faith, and I hadn't told anyone I was going to do it. The book was written by a God-fearing man who had actually obeyed God's call to live by faith, and he founded the China Mission on the strength of his obedience. There and then I determined in my heart that I would give up all I owned, and trust in God to provide. Now it couldn't be avoided, I told my wife about what the Lord had said.

The weeks passed and I disposed of the very last of our savings. I still hadn't asked anyone to fund my work, and unlike some Christians who ask a church to finance them once they make a decision to live by faith, I never did. I remember the day when I drew our very last £5 out of the bank as clearly as if it were yesterday. I prayed, 'Don't let me down Lord, we must feed the children!' and I handed the last of our money to my wife.

There were passages from Scripture on which I relied from this day onwards; they were a source of strength then, and throughout my ministry and life;

'Do not worry about anything, but in everything by prayer and supplication, with thanksgiving, let your requests be made known unto God'[12] And, *'My God shall supply all your need according to his riches in glory by Christ Jesus.'*[13]

'For what shall it profit a man, if he shall gain the whole world, and lose his own soul?'[14]

I was being greatly blessed at the Evangelical Free Church, and I'd also been helping the Gideons distribute Bibles in hotels and prisons, but I knew God had a bigger job for me to do.

The months passed until one day in 1958 I felt the Lord speak to me very clearly, saying, 'I have called you to preach.' Those were the words I heard, no more or less.

'Who to? Where?' I prayed, desperate to learn more. But no further answer came. I spent time thinking about the call and assumed God would want me to preach to businessmen like I myself had been, or maybe to students – well-bred, educated people certainly.

While I was still waiting for guidance on the call to preach, a very godly man I knew invited me to come with him to preach in the open air.

'What do you mean?' I asked, feeling nervous.

'To stand in the street and preach the Gospel,' he said.

'Oh, I couldn't possibly do that! Never!'

'Yes you can,' he replied.

So I prayed and prayed and asked the Lord to tell me what He wanted me to do. And the answer came, 'I don't want you to go with that man, I want you to go on your own, to the green in front of the Anglican church and preach the Gospel.'

'Oh no!' I said, because this was something too difficult and dreadful to contemplate. I was a member of our local parish council, and it simply wasn't done to stand in the open air in the village preaching, people would assume I was a madman.

I spent a long time trying to pluck up the courage to obey God's call, and didn't dare tell anybody, not even my own wife.

The Lord gave me a clear call from Romans 10 verses 13-17, *'Whosoever calls upon the name of the Lord shall be saved. How then shall they call on him in whom they have not believed?*

And how shall they believe in him of whom they have not heard? And how shall they hear without a preacher?

And how shall they preach, except they be sent? As it is written, how beautiful are the feet of them that preach the Gospel of peace and bring glad tidings of good things!'

After thinking about these words long and hard, I went to the village green and tried to preach, but hadn't got the courage to begin, and walked away feeling very despondent.

The next week I tried again, with the same result, I simply wasn't brave enough to speak out and preach the Gospel.

On the third week, I went back to the green and asked God to give me the words, knowing I couldn't make myself do it. I hadn't prepared anything to say, and just stood waiting on God. An elderly lady was waiting at the bus stop, with a man close beside her on the seat. Then the words came, God gave me the inspiration. I don't remember what I preached, but I do remember what happened next, the old lady burst into tears, and the man on the seat took his hat off and got down on his knees when he heard God speaking through me. There was so much power around us, and we all felt it.

After that, my confidence began to blossom and I was ready to preach for the Lord. Not long afterwards I heard another call, 'Go back to your old village of Brenchley and hold an evangelistic mission in the village hall for three weeks.'

My newly found confidence began to ebb away at once, because one of the two hundred pubs I had managed on the Whitbread Board of Directors was right opposite that village hall.

It was winter, and one Saturday night, soon after that call, I was due to give a testimony at a C of E Church in Tunbridge Wells. As we no longer had a car, I couldn't afford the ticket for a bus or train, and the Lord had provided an old push-bike. The road from our house to the church passed down through a dark wood, and I had to peddle back that way late in the evening after the meeting. It was a very dark, cold night and as I cycled through the middle of the wood, I heard a voice saying, 'You're crazy - absolutely stark-raving mad. You've got a wife and children and you're giving everything away, you're irresponsible and crazy.' As I heard the words, a cold gnawing fear took possession of me, and a sudden doubt that I was doing the right thing. For the first time since my conversion I felt utterly terrified. I'm convinced now it was the Devil's voice I heard, and his despair that I felt.

But then I felt the Lord come into my despair and heard Him speak words of deep comfort, 'Don't worry. Trust me, I am with you.' In an instant, the fear and despair left me, and I felt strong enough to cycle home.

People have asked me whether I ever doubted or gave up on God, and that night is the closest I ever came.

So there I was, newly committed to live by faith, whatever it entailed, and called to hold an evangelistic mission in my old village of Brenchley. I had decided to begin the three week mission on a Monday, everything was advertised, but there was an additional complication – how would I get there without money for the fare?

Early on that Monday morning when I was still in bed, my little daughter Sally heard the letterbox clang and ran downstairs. She brought me an envelope and inside I found a letter of encouragement from a woman who told me she wanted to support the evangelistic mission. With it was a ten shilling note 'for my needs'. I held up the money and stared at it in wonder. I hadn't asked anybody for donations, and not a soul knew of my decision to live by faith, but God had sent the first piece of hard evidence that His promise to provide was real. I had it right there in my hand. That proof of God's loving providence gave me the confidence I needed to set out for Brenchley and preach the Gospel in a place I'd been afraid to go. And since that very first gift, His miraculous provision has never stopped, and continues to this day. All I have to do is trust.

My dread of holding the mission right opposite one of the pubs I had managed proved groundless. The Lord made a path for me and the mission was a huge success. The greatest miracle of all came from the place I had feared most, for not only did the pub landlady support my efforts, but she came to hear me preach, and before the end of my three weeks, she was converted right outside her pub. God is very gracious, He showed that my fears were unfounded, then turned them into a blessing. More than forty years later, I feel the joy of it.

After the success of this mission, I felt the Lord call me to hold similar evangelistic missions in other villages around Kent. I had no backing from any church or organisation, and every step I took was founded on prayer. I learned to rely on the Lord absolutely for our needs, and to trust that his Holy Spirit would incline the hearts of people to give.

But trusting was never easy, and my human nature put doubts and fears in the way. One morning in the very early stages of living by faith, we had used our last tea, bread and milk and there was nothing to give the children for breakfast. My wife struggled on nobly. Although she didn't share my faith, she had put her hand up at one of our meetings to accept Jesus as her Saviour.

But that morning all my trust disappeared and I felt full of anxiety for my family who, for the first time in their lives, had nothing to eat.

So I opened my Bible and asked the Lord what I

should do, and I read the words, '*Seek ye first the Kingdom of God and his righteousness, and all the other things shall be added unto you.*'[15].

I understood at once what God was saying to me, that I must put Him first, and everything else would follow. So I prayed for the Holy Spirit to move my heart completely towards the Kingdom of God.

From then on, for the two years from 1958 to 1960, I went from village to village, seventeen of them in all, holding a mission in each. In that time I covered most villages twice, Horsmonden, Brenchley, Goudhurst, Marden and many more. God called me with a verse from 2 Corinthians 11 v 28, '*That which cometh upon me daily (is) the care of all the churches.*'

First I asked God to tell me where He wanted me to go, then I would contact the village hall secretary and request the use of their room for an evangelistic mission. I had leaflets printed with times and venues, and notified the police in advance. In every case the village agreed to have me, and never once in two years was I asked for a penny to hire the building. That was a good thing as I wouldn't have been able to pay!

I knew the Lord didn't want me to appeal for funds, and I never did, even refusing to hold a collection at the end of my meetings, but every time I left, the money was there. The agenda was simple, we sang together, read from God's word, and I preached the Gospel, then made an opportunity for people to come forward for prayer and commitment.

The money kept coming in, always anonymously, and always the right amount to provide for our needs, feed the children, and get me to the next village. I preached outside in the open air on village greens, stood on street corners, and knocked on every door to share God's word with the villagers. Whenever I needed a bed for the night, the Lord raised up a place for me to stay. During those years, many, many people accepted Christ into their lives, and I saw people blessed and strengthened. God supplied our every need and I sensed a deep movement of God's spirit in those middle-class English villages.

But another morning came when we drank the last of the tea and ate our last slices of bread, and I was afraid my children would go hungry. There was nothing left in the cupboard. But this time I didn't hesitate or panic, just got down on my knees and prayed that the Lord would send me five pounds. In those days five pounds was enough to feed a family for a week.

In faith I started my prayer, 'Heavenly Father, I come to you in Jesus' name…' but got no further, because I heard something drop through the letterbox on to the mat.

I walked to the door and picked up an envelope, and inside found a piece of paper, with the words, *'Before they call I will answer, and while they are yet speaking, I will hear.'*[16] And wrapped inside the letter was a five pound note. Miracles like this became a way of life for me, and to this day I don't know who gave to us, we just received what we needed through the leading of God's Holy Spirit, no more or less, but always right on time.

One evening my wife prepared our evening meal of meat and vegetables, but we had no bread left, so when we sat down at the table we simply prayed, 'Almighty God, would you send us a loaf of bread?' Then I gave thanks to the Lord for the food just as if we had already got a loaf of bread. I'd just finished praying and the doorbell rang - two Christian friends were standing outside.

The man said, 'We were out for a drive and thought we'd drop by to say hello, and we felt led to bring you this.' And he handed me a loaf of fresh bread. Praise the Lord!

Once the Lord woke a woman in America at 2a.m. to tell her to send money to me. She'd never met me, but the Lord laid me on her heart.

So I was beginning to learn the true meaning of living by faith. The Bible says, *'Faith is the substance of things hopeful, or evidence of things not seen.'* [17]

The meaning of this verse became clear to me during these first years of trusting God to provide. If we can see or touch something, or turn it over in our hands, then we don't need faith to believe in it. True faith is believing what you cannot see or touch. Millions of people across the world are called and saved by the blood of Jesus, but only a tiny fraction of those are called to live by faith for financial provision. When people like me are called, God has a very specific reason and purpose.

But it wouldn't be true to say I never struggled – I did. During those first years of living by faith, God gave me one more command. Before my conversion I had been a successful steeplechaser. Although I'd long since given up the cars and horses, I still had the silver cups I'd won for races, and they meant a lot to me. For years my mother had lovingly polished each cup, and the collection had pride of place on her sideboard at home.

One day I heard the Lord say to me, 'Give everything up!' and I thought to myself – That's OK, I've given everything up, except my riding cups. But I heard the Lord say again, 'Give everything up, I want those cups as well!'

That really grieved me, and I thought of the love my mother had lavished on the cups, and how much they symbolised the worldly successes of my past life. I spoke to an elderly pastor who was deeply steeped in the Lord, and he told me, 'It's no good praying for money if you haven't given up everything of any worth.'

It hurt me more than losing my money, cars or horses,

but I sold the cups, and the money was what we really needed. It was the hardest thing I ever gave up for the Lord. And the pain proved why it was so important to let go of the tie that still bound me to my past.

Although I never appealed for money, or publicised the fact that we were living by faith, a few local people became aware of my ministry. Just before Christmas in 1960, I sat opening the post. Inside several cards I found good wishes and an occasional five pound note for the Lord's work. Inside one I found £10 - a lot of money in 1960. The last envelope contained a cheque, with another £10, and I thought – praise the Lord! Then I looked at the amount more closely and saw that it was actually £100.

'Glory be to God!' I said aloud, but as I peered at the longhand script, I saw it was made out not for £100, but an incredible one thousand pounds!

I was amazed - here in my hand was an anonymous cheque, signed by someone I'd never heard of, and made out in my name for a thousand pounds.

The cheque came from Lloyds Bank in Cranbrook, and I decided to visit my bank to find out where it had come from. The cashier said, 'I'll try and find out for you,' and disappeared. When she came back to the window she said, 'The signature is one of the staff at the Cranbrook branch of Lloyds. The bank was instructed to send you the cheque but not divulge the giver. That's why it was signed by one of their staff.'

'Is there no way of finding out who sent it?' I asked.

'I'm afraid not, the donor insisted on confidentiality.'

It was a miraculous and wonderful gift, and my mind continued to play over the mystery - I wished I knew who had given so much for my work.

Almost a year later, while I was walking in Goudhurst, I met a friend who said, 'Did you by any chance receive a large cheque last Christmas?'

'Yes I did.'

'In case you're interested, I have the name and address of the person who gave it,' he said.

I was very interested indeed, and called at the address soon afterwards.

The door was answered by an elderly man.

'Good day,' I said, 'I think you and I have something in common, we're both born again.'

'I'm not born again,' he said firmly.

'My name's Pastor John Lywood.'

'Ah, then I assume somebody's told you about the thousand pounds I sent you last Christmas?'

'Well if you're not a Christian and we've never met, then why did you send me so much money?'

'Because I was in St Mary's Church on Armistice Day and you were preaching,' he said, 'and it struck me that instead of speaking a whole lot of twaddle, you preached the truth, so I sent you a thousand pounds for Christmas.'

I was awe-struck at the power of the Holy Spirit that had moved this stranger, not even a believer, to respond to my preaching with such a magnanimous gift. I thanked the man and went home with joy in my heart, seeing how my obedience to God's call to live by faith was being rewarded. It has continued throughout my long life, and to this day I'm richly blessed, although I own nothing, and have no home of my own. Praise God!

Upon this mountain shall the hand of the Lord rest

*F*or the two years after my first mission in Brenchley, I was always directed by God in response to prayer. When I prayed about my next destination I followed the same method, spreading open the Ordnance Survey map of Kent, and laying the Bible on my knee. As I prayed for guidance I opened the Bible and, without fail, a verse or word would spring off the paper and tell me where to go next.

To give an example, one mission was held at a village on a hill. After I had preached and worked there for three weeks, I sat down to ask God for guidance.

I prayed, 'Do you want me to stay here another week Lord, or move on?' I let my Bible fall open, and immediately the words jumped out, *'You have been on this mountain long enough, turn northwards.'* [18]

So I traced the northerly line on my map, found the next village to the north, and moved on to preach there the next week.

Early one morning in 1960, during a mission in Goudhurst, I was praying for guidance, when suddenly, and with tremendous power, the Lord gave me a verse, *'Upon this mountain shall the hand of the Lord rest.'* [19] At that time I didn't understand the reference to the Moabites which followed, and it was to be many months before the full impact of those words was revealed.

But I certainly understood verse 10. Goudhurst is built on a hill, and I knew God was asking me to stay and build a church in the village. In my ignorance I assumed He meant me to build with bricks and mortar, and literally make a new building.

The first thing I did was book the village hall for a

regular time-slot every Sunday morning, and after these Sunday services started, I realised I wasn't being asked to construct a building, but found a church of people.

The Sunday service became a permanent booking. At first very few locals came to the hall on the crossroads beside the village pond, but gradually, week after week, the number in the congregation grew as the Gospel was preached in the hall, on the village green, and in the two housing estates. We called ourselves the Goudhurst Evangelical Free Church and ran on the same basis as many other free churches.

At exactly the same time that I had the word from Isaiah about founding the Goudhurst church, I had another powerful lead from the Lord. It happened while I was pedalling along the country lanes on my old push-bike.

It was a day like any other, until I cycled into Brenchley village, the place I had previously worked, lived and preached. As I approached the village hall, I had an overpowering sensation of blessing fall upon the ground on and around the hall, like an aura, a blanket of spiritual blessing. The sensation was strongest over the building itself as I passed by, and then lifted completely after I passed. God placed in my mind the certain conviction that I must found a church in Brenchley, along the same lines as the one in Goudhurst.

Again there was no congregation to preach to, but I trusted God to resolve it by His grace, and booked the hall indefinitely. So I preached in the two village halls and two housing estates every single Sunday, a ministry which was to continue for 35 years until 1995.

From the very earliest days, we saw miracles in the new churches at Goudhurst and Brenchley. Immediately after we began, a new church member had made me aware of a little baby in our neighbourhood whose mother was worn out with worry because her child was an epileptic. The poor baby was having fits twice every day. The man in our congregation told me the mother couldn't carry on any longer and he invited her to our Sunday service so we could pray for the child. He encouraged her to come and she agreed.

The next Sunday morning, when we were half way through the breaking of bread, I saw a young woman walk into the church, carrying a baby in her arms. As soon as she put her foot on the floor of the church, the child went into a deep epileptic fit. I broke off from the service and went up to the mother asking, 'Can I pray for you?' and she was too upset to reply.

'Just close your eyes,' I said, 'and I'll claim the power of the blood of Jesus over the Devil and all his works, and pray for protection for your little baby.'

So I laid my hand above the child and asked the Lord for power and protection. Before our very eyes, the fit immediately left the child's body.

I was powerfully reminded of the descriptions of children healed by Jesus, and I've often thought of the biblical explanation of evil spirits. But whatever the cause and effect may be, it's true that the child never had another fit and was completely healed. The mother herself came back and told us of the miraculous healing God had done before our eyes.

Baptism was an important part of the work of our new churches. Nowhere in God's word in the Bible is there any mention of infant christening or confirmation. Jesus said to his disciples, 'Go out and preach the Gospel, those who believe and all who are baptised shall be saved.'[20]

It's clear to everybody that a little baby cannot repent or believe, therefore infant baptism is quite obviously wrong. But what's the alternative? Jesus was baptised in the River Jordan as an adult, so when we get baptised we follow Jesus through the water of baptism. He was never christened, he was dedicated as a baby, and that's exactly what we do, dedicate the little children.

The first time I dedicated a baby, the Holy Spirit did the most wonderful, powerful thing. The child leapt in my arms as the Holy Spirit came down upon it, and I was reminded of when the child leapt in Mary's womb when she greeted Elizabeth. Every child I've dedicated has always leapt in my arms, confirming the true doctrine of dedication followed in later years by baptism by immersion in water, the way the Bible describes.

There are several reasons why we should be baptised, first we should be born again, second to follow Jesus through the waters of baptism, and third it's the outward sign showing our sins are forgiven. The water will never take our sins away, it can't wash away one sin - only the blood of Jesus can do that, but as we go under the water, it's a sign that we've already had our sins forgiven. As we come up out of the water, that's a sign we've started a new life following Jesus. And baptism strengthens the church, as a witness and testimony to God's saving grace.

One of the most remarkable miracles I ever witnessed happened at this time while we were living in Crowborough and founding the two new churches.

I'd just returned home and found a group of people in our house. Then the woman who lived opposite us rushed in sobbing, 'He's gone, he's gone!' She was in a terrible state because her husband had just died.

Everyone in my house tried to comfort her, by hugging her and praying. Suddenly the Lord said to me, 'Leave all that, don't take any part in it.'

Somehow I was propelled, and found myself walking across the road to the woman's house opposite. I knocked on the door, no-one answered, so I went straight in, looked around the downstairs rooms, couldn't see anybody, went upstairs, opened the first bedroom door, couldn't see anybody, opened the second, and found the woman's husband, lying dead on the bed.

There was no doubt whatsoever that he was completely dead - he wasn't breathing and had no pulse, so I thought the best thing was to kneel down and commit his soul to the Lord. The man was a strict Baptist. So I knelt down and began to pray.

Immediately the Lord said, 'Stand up on your feet, lay your hands on him and I'll raise him up!'

There was nobody in the house but me. I stood up, prayed, and laid hands on the man. As I prayed, I felt a terrific power go through my body, an incredible force. Underneath my hands, the man's chest moved as he began to breathe. Then he opened his eyes, and looked round as if he didn't know whether he was in heaven or earth, saw me and without a word, got up and dressed. As he finished dressing, I heard voices of his wife and the doctor on the stairs.

When she came into the room, his wife took one look and fainted. The doctor stared at me and said, 'It's a miracle.'

Even though I'd seen this with my own eyes, I could hardly believe it, and couldn't take it in. That man lived for another seven years.

Another sign of encouragement for our new churches happened after I'd taken an evening service at Goudhurst. My push-bike had given up and I faced a long, cold winter's walk home in the dark. I set off downhill and the night air was black as pitch.

As I walked I prayed, 'Lord, please send me a lift.' Several cars hummed by without stopping, and eventually a man drew up and offered to drive me to Sevenoaks, which was close to our home. After he dropped me I'd walked no more than ten yards when another vehicle stopped and the driver asked where I was heading.

'I'm going that way, jump in,' he said, 'Has your car broken down?'

'Oh no, I'm a minister of God, and I just pray and trust God for lifts,' I explained.

His next question surprised me, 'So how do you live?'

'By faith.'

'Well praise the Lord! Then I must tell you what happened to me tonight, it's a miracle. I'm a believer myself and run an electrical shop in Sevenoaks. Recently I fell behind with my tithing to charity, and the Lord corrected me about it, so for the past six weeks I've been giving wherever God prompted me, because he's really prospered my business. Although I didn't understand why, I felt God wanted me to keep a little bit back, and this evening while I was sitting at home by the fire, for no reason at all the Lord said to me, 'Take the last ten pounds of your tithe, get in your car and drive round Sevenoaks.' So that's what I did and here you are.'

And he reached inside his pocket and handed me a ten pound note.

'This is the last bit of money the Lord wanted me to give.'

That donation provided enough food for my family for two weeks and was a miraculous encouragement.

By now the Lord had given me another word about caring for down and outs, *'Show them the proof of my love, show them the proof.'*[21]

That verse inspired me to visit people in trouble, either in court or prison - to show them God's love.

I didn't have the money for a car or train fares, but the Lord had said to me, 'Walk down the road and pray and you will get lifts.'

People used to call it hitch-hiking, but I never hitch-hiked, just prayed and held my hand up. I never once thumbed, but cars just used to stop, whether I raised my hand or not. As soon as I got out of one car, I thanked the Lord for the lift He'd already provided, and prayed for the next one. Every time. People asked me, 'How can you guarantee to be in a place at a certain time when you're relying on lifts?' But in all the years I did it, I was never a minute late, even for court.

After Fred Scruton had been converted and smartened up, one day I said, 'You can come with me today Freddie if you like.'

'I'd love to.'

I was due at Greenwich Magistrates court to speak for a man at 10a.m. and this was just before 9a.m.

Fred and I set off from Tunbridge Wells, walking and praying and got a lift to the roundabout outside Sevenoaks. There wasn't a lot of traffic, and suddenly a fine, expensive Daimler approached, and the driver gave us a look as if we were dirt and drove on.

'We'll not get a lift from him,' I said to Fred.

Amazingly, he drove only a hundred yards along the road and stopped, reversed and said in a very haughty voice, 'Do you want a lift?'

'That's very kind of you, thank you very much indeed.'

I think he was amazed to hear that I spoke well. We got in.

'Do you usually go around the countryside thumbing lifts?' he asked.

I said 'To be perfectly honest I never thumb a lift, but pray to God and trust that I'll get one.'

'Good heavens alive, you mean you pray for lifts? That alters the whole thing, have you had breakfast? I'll take you and buy some.'

The change in him was amazing.

I said, 'That's very kind but we've had breakfast.'

'Where are you going?'

'To Greenwich Magistrates court.'

'What for?'

'To speak for a man.'

'Then I'll drive you there. Tell me more about what you do.'

He turned out to be the Managing Director of TV Southern and he drove us straight to the door of the court bang on time.

After we'd finished, Freddie said to me, 'Look - we've got here, but how are we going to get home? We've got miles to walk. It's relatively easy to get lifts from the country into town, but not so easy to get lifts the other way.'

'God will provide,' I said.

At that minute a solicitor came out of the court, I knew him slightly and asked, 'Are you by any chance going back to Tunbridge Wells?'

'Yes.'

'You couldn't give us a lift could you?'

'Certainly, jump in,' and away we went.

It was all by faith, I never had anything planned. God took us there and back, this time and many others.

There was only one time in my life when God didn't provide me with a lift. It happened during the very hard winter of 1963, after I'd led an evening service at Benenden near Ashford. We finished at ten o'clock, and it's a long way back to Crowborough without a car.

I set out on my feet in the direction of home and it was really, bitterly cold. I felt sure the Lord would send me a lift soon, but for the first time ever, none came, and I was getting colder and colder, and more exhausted.

I had another three miles to walk to reach the main road. It was past one a.m. and I thought, 'I can't go any further - if I'm going to die, then I'm going to die,' but I knew that if I sat or lay down, it would be the end of me.

So I forced myself to walk to the main road, where I saw approaching headlights and just prayed, 'Lord, please let that one stop.'

The car pulled over, but I was frozen stiff and couldn't speak. I truly thought I was going to die. The driver dropped me in Tunbridge Wells where I got another lift from a lorry. I was so cold I can't describe it to you, I thought I'd never get warm again. I slept for most of the next day, and asked the Lord why He had let this happen to me.

He replied, 'That was an apostolic walk like Paul went through – when he was beaten, flogged and ship-wrecked.' It was the only time He didn't answer my prayer for a lift.

I'd like to record an incident from this period concerning the Holy Spirit. One afternoon my wife, myself, Bobby Freer and my daughter Sally were in the kitchen. We decided to pray and I could feel the Holy Spirit falling among us.

Suddenly without a word of warning, my little girl who was eight years old, started to pray with a loud voice using words she was totally ignorant of; 'Advocate, mediator, atonement and justification.' She prayed in this way for a full ten minutes in an adult voice with wonderful messages coming through.

Then she clapped her little hands together and stopped. I was absolutely staggered to have heard these words coming out of her - straight from the Holy Spirit.

When I went to say goodnight to her in bed, she was back to normal and said the same ordinary childish prayers she'd always said, 'God bless Mummy and God bless Daddy.' For those few minutes the Holy Spirit had spoken to us through her. Sally can't remember that now, but we never forgot it, I was awe-struck.

The next part of my story is very, very difficult for

me to tell. I came home one night in 1964 and found my wife had gone, with the three children, leaving a note to say she had left me.

We had been through some very hard times, and although God had supplied our needs wonderfully, there's no doubt she'd had to go through more privations and difficulties than most people ever have to.

This is very hard to say, but I believe that if I had loved her as I should have done, then she wouldn't have gone. The Lord only revealed that to me years later and I had a lot of repenting to do. This is part of my life which I don't want to speak about.

John Wesley once said about his own wife, 'I did not ask her to leave and I will not ask her to return.' Those words made a lot of sense to me. So I found myself alone, and had to rely on God even more.

For the next five years, night and day, in winter and summer, rain, snow and ice, I went all round Kent simply praying and trusting the Lord and getting lifts from place to place. I always dressed smartly in a collar and tie and carried nothing but my Bible.

The conversions and healings I saw were manifold, and by God's grace I was able to preach the Gospel to lorry drivers, commercial travellers, and businessmen, planting seeds in their lives.

One day I set off on foot to visit a man the Lord had put on my heart, and I prayed for a lift. After I'd walked half a mile a car stopped.

The driver was going part way to my destination and offered me a lift.

I told him, 'I'm a minister of God, I pray and lifts come along.'

He was quiet when I said that.

When he dropped me off I thanked him very much.

'Just a minute, before you go,' he said, taking out his

wallet and giving me a £5 note.

'That's very kind,' I said.

'Not really, it's you who's been kind to me, I was a back-slider and meeting you in this wonderful way has brought me back to God. Thank you.'

I was once offered a lift by a Roman Catholic priest near Canterbury. As I got in, the Lord said, 'Witness to him!'

So I just came out with it, and told him I believed the Roman Catholic church was flawed.

Do you know what he did? Jammed the brakes on, turned absolutely blue with anger, opened the door and yelled, 'Get out!'

'You've got no need to be annoyed just because I said that.'

Through gritted teeth he said, 'After what you've said about the organisation I belong to!'

'I said what I believe.' Then the Holy Spirit fell on me and I said, 'But it doesn't mean you're condemned.'

He burst into tears, grabbed my arm, and said, 'Please pray for me.' So his reaction proved I'd said what God wanted me to.

On another occasion I had a lift with a Roman Catholic priest, and wasn't feeling very much in the spirit, and didn't witness to him properly. When I got out, the Lord rebuked me.

So when I met the Roman Catholic priest walking in Goudhurst I was more fired up. I said, 'Morning Mr Jones.'

He said 'Father Jones if you please.'

'Mr Jones if you please.'

'Who do you think you are? Who do you make yourself out to be? The vicar calls me Father Jones, the Methodist minister calls me Father Jones, so why can't you?'

'Because the Lord forbids me.'

'What do you mean?'

'The Bible says, *'Call no preacher Father, you have one Father.'*[22]

He said, 'I never knew that was in the Bible! Have you got ten minutes to spare? Could you come back and talk to me?'

So I went with him and preached the Gospel for nearly an hour.

When I finished he said, 'Correct me if I'm wrong, but you're saying we're all sinners, we're all on our way to hell, but if we believe that Jesus took our sins in his own body on the cross and rose from the dead, and we receive him as Saviour, then we'll be saved. Is that what you're saying?'

'Yes, just that.'

'Too easy. You've left out good works.'

'Well good works won't save us. We do good works, not to get saved, but because we're already saved.'

That's how our meeting ended, and I left it with the Lord.

Should I have buried the truth just to avoid offending someone? It isn't just the Catholic church that needs correction, I believe the Church of England is an apostate church, its theology is often wrong, it christens infants, and ordains homosexuals, and if we believe in the Bible, how can that possibly be right?

But the bottom line is that God loves the sinner. Not the sin, but the sinner - and we're all sinners, every one.

During the years of walking the roads I felt completely free, and loved every minute of it. I've never felt so free in all my life as I did then, with no money, and no car, just trusting the Lord for everything. It felt like heaven.

One beautiful night, at about one o'clock in the morning, I was on my way home and heard a car coming very fast. I prayed it would stop, but it passed me at about a hundred miles an hour. It was such a lovely night that you could have heard a pin drop, and I thought - well that car's gone.

About a mile up the road ahead, I heard the car stop, turn, come back, pass me again, turn and come alongside me.

'Did you want a lift?' said the driver, winding down his window.

'That's very kind, as a matter of fact I'm a minister of God and I always pray for a lift.'

'I know.'

'Where did we meet?'

'We've never met.'

'So how did you know I was a minister of God?'

'Because as I passed, fifty yards either side of you was a great aura of wonderful peace.'

When I told a different driver that I was a minister, he said, 'I'll give you a lift but I want no preaching or talking about God and no talking about the Bible. If you do, that door opens and out you get.'

'That's OK,' I said, 'It's very nice of you to give me a lift.'

'I'm only too pleased to help.'

'It's a lovely day isn't it?'

'Yes lovely.'

'It's a gift from God,' I said.

And from that moment he let me talk about the Lord without stopping me.

This next memory is so incredible, I can hardly believe it happened. I'd had nothing to eat on a very hot day, and was tired and very thirsty - all I wanted was a cup of tea and sandwich to keep me going. Suddenly I remembered a Christian family nearby and decided to go and knock on their door.

The Lord said to me, 'You're not going so you can minister to the people, you're after a cup of tea and a sandwich.'

'You're right Lord,' I said, turning back in the other direction. After I'd walked ten yards, a lorry pulled up and said, 'Do you want a lift mate?'

'Yes, thanks.' I never said a single word about God or my ministry, I felt low.

The driver put his hand in his pocket and said, 'That's for you,' passing me half a crown - which was a lot of money in those days.

I tried to refuse but he said, 'Have it. I'm going to drop you off in East Malling, then you should walk down the road, knock on the third door on the right and ask them for a cup of tea and a sandwich.'

This was extraordinary, and I assumed he must be describing a café.

When he dropped me off, I walked three doors down, knocked, and a middle-aged woman answered as if she had been expecting me. I'd never seen her in my life before.

'Come in and sit down,' she said and brought me a cup of tea and a pile of sandwiches although I never asked for anything. I asked how much I owed her and she said, 'Nothing.'

That's exactly how it happened, it was awesome. There was no human explanation, and I'll never know whether the lorry driver was an angel or a man. It all happened because I turned round in trust, and admitted I was wrong. Do you know – those sandwiches tasted sweeter than anything, because I was obedient.

Another experience like that happened in Maidstone where I was ministering to the dossers. Again it was scorching hot, and I was flagging from heat and hunger. As I was walking along Stone Street I felt my attention drawn to one house and heard the Lord say to me, 'Knock on that door.'

I did as I was told, and a middle-aged woman answered.

'Excuse me,' I said, 'Would you be kind enough to give me a glass of water because I'm so very hot?'

'Certainly,' she said, and disappeared indoors. While I waited, a man came past me into the house.

'Don't keep this chap waiting on the doorstep!' he called to his wife, and invited me inside. Completely unprompted, he asked 'Would you like something to eat?' and proceeded to make me a big plate of poached eggs on toast.

I never saw them again. Amazing.

Although my life was a world away from my past, the Lord gave me occasional reminders of that past. An old-boy from my public school was now a farmer in Horsmonden, and we remained in touch. Not long after I'd begun living by faith he spoke to me of a friend of his, also from Sherborne School, who'd fallen on hard times because of his drink problem. He was living in Birmingham and selling papers on the street, and when I heard his story, I decided to find him and help if I could.

I set off on my feet from Kent with sixpence in my pocket, and began to walk towards Birmingham. When I felt really hungry I bought myself 6d worth of chips, which reduced me to nothing. I was offered lifts most of the way, but by nightfall I was still thirty or forty miles short of Birmingham, and it was a bitterly cold winter's night. As I walked along the bypass, the frost was already severe, and I became colder and colder. Cars whizzed past at 70 miles an hour and I prayed again that the Lord would send a lift.

In the end a man pulled up and I was thoroughly glad to climb into his warm car.

'Where are you going?' he asked.

'Into Birmingham.'

'Well, I'll take you there.'

'Thank you very much. I'm a minister of God and simply pray and trust God for lifts to get from place to place,' I explained with my stock phrase for every driver who stopped.

'Well now you've said that, I'm going to tell you something very extraordinary. I'm a salesman and tonight I was in bed in a hotel many miles north of here. Suddenly as I lay in bed I heard a voice saying, 'Get up, dress and drive home.' And I thought to myself – that's ridiculous, tomorrow morning I have an appointment near this hotel, so I must be dreaming. But the voice became so persistent that I had to get up, dress and drive home. And now I know why I had to do it - to give you a lift into Birmingham.'

'Which you did, Amen,' I said, and never forgot that salesman.

I arrived at the address my friend had given me at three a.m. - far too late to wake the man, so I walked the streets until seven o'clock and then knocked on the man's door. We'd never met and I knew he wouldn't recognise me, so I introduced myself as a friend of his friend, 'He runs a hop farm in Kent now, and all three of us used to be at Sherborne.'

'Cor, that's good of you to come all this way to see me. Where did you park your car?'

'I don't have a car, I simply rely on God to provide lifts.'

'Have you got any money for the meter, so I can put the electricity on and make us a cup of coffee? I've got some coffee and fivepence, but the meter takes sixpence.'

Suddenly the situation struck me as very funny. Here we were, two ex-public schoolboys, without sixpence between us for the electricity to make a cup of coffee.

I said, 'What about asking next door for the money?'

'No we can't, I already owe them so much money and haven't paid them back.'

'They'll lend it if I ask,' I said and knocked on the door.

I tapped on the door and said to the man, 'We've got 5d and we need a penny to get the electricity going for a cup of coffee.

The neighbour handed me the money and we had our drink and I ministered to him as best I could.

By the time I set off for home I was very cold, weak and hungry, and hadn't eaten since the chips twenty-four hours earlier, and it was a long walk until a lorry stopped. The driver took one look at me and without a word, he pushed a packet of biscuits across the dashboard to me. By God's grace I reached home.

You shall bring forth fruit and your fruit shall remain

*I*n the early 1960's our little church at Goudhurst had begun by thriving, but the local people eventually rejected the Gospel. Our fledgling congregations were formed mainly from middle-class local families, but after initial growth in the first couple of years, numbers had begun to decline.

Once a year in Goudhurst I would see lots of fierce, dark characters driving into the village in vans, and I was afraid of them. As we came out of church one Sunday morning I asked a member of church, 'Who are all these people?'

'They're gypsies from the camp. They're here for the hop-picking.'

I thanked the Lord that I wasn't called to preach to people like that!

The next year at the same time, the gypsies returned to the area in their vans and lorries. Although I'd worked with down and outs, I was genuinely afraid of the gypsies, because they looked hard and defiant. Again I thanked God that He didn't want me to minister to rough people like them, and immediately heard God speak into my mind, 'I want you to preach to the gypsies.'

My heart missed a beat and I prayed hard, 'How can I get any message across to people who have no education, and are tough and rough? I was educated at public school! They wouldn't understand a word I say, and I certainly wouldn't understand them. So I can't do it.'

But God wouldn't leave it there. I'd developed a fascination for these dark people, and the Holy Spirit kept on moving my heart toward them. The more I prayed and thought about the gypsies, I had to admit that local people's hearts had begun to harden against us, and all we were trying to do in our little churches in Goudhurst and Brenchley. The locals were drifting away.

It was then the Lord revealed the meaning of verse 11 in Isaiah 25, just after the word that had called me to found the new church, *'and he shall bring down their pride.'* The villagers were like the Moabites, whose pride prevented them from hearing God's word in their midst. The Holy Spirit moved me to understand that although the locals were rejecting the Gospel, the gypsies would embrace it. So eventually I couldn't stay away from them any longer.

This was the incident that started it all, and it's one of the most important in my life. Just outside Goudhurst the gypsies had made their camp on a large hop farm. I prayed to the Lord for courage and decided to take a leap of faith, and set off to preach the Gospel in the camp. From a distance I could see about twenty-five vans, countless children running about and Alsation dogs barking.

'Well Lord, I said I'd go,' I prayed as I walked down the lane towards the site. Immediately a gypsy came up to me on a tractor.

'Where the hell are you going?' he barked. It suddenly occurred to me he'd seen my suit and tie and might think I was a plain clothed policeman. I paused and he jumped down from his tractor.

'I'm coming to speak to these people,' I said.

'Oh no you're not!' he yelled, and held up his hand as if he was about to strike me.

I was at a loss for words, and from nowhere the Lord put a phrase into my head, 'I'm sorry, I've got to. I'm under orders.'

'Orders?' he snarled, 'Who from?'

'Almighty God.'

The gypsy turned pale before my eyes, and didn't say

another word, he just stood aside to let me pass.

A caravan was drawn up beside the first gate at the end of the lane. Outside, sitting on the step, was one of the swarthy gypsies I'd seen in Goudhurst, with two little children playing in the dirt.

'Good afternoon,' I said.

'Hhmm.'

'I'm a minister of God and I've come to read the Bible to you,' I said. As he didn't reply, I opened John's Gospel and began to read a passage aloud. I could tell he wasn't listening, but after a minute he butted in, 'Can you pray?'

'Yes, I can pray.'

'You see these two kids, their mother has left them and me, will you pray she'll come back?'

'Just close your eyes and I'll pray. Almighty Father, wherever this woman is, will you send her home? Please send her back home to this man and her children. Amen.'

When I opened my eyes, the big burly gypsy had tears running down his cheeks.

'I'll be back tomorrow,' I said and left the site.

I returned at the same time next day. As I walked up to the van, I suspected a miracle had taken place, because I saw a young woman sitting with the same two children. When we spoke, she told me she was the man's wife and had come back to him.

'What time yesterday did you pray I'd come back?' she asked me.

'It was two o'clock.'

'I was sitting in my mother's house in London and looked up at the clock at two o'clock, and a voice in my head said to me, 'Go back to your husband.'

It was the very moment I had prayed.

Her husband was overjoyed and slapped me on the back as if I were an old friend.

'I'm going to introduce you to all the others,' he

promised, and that was my opening into the world of the gypsies.

That miraculous response to prayer spread like wildfire through the gypsies of Kent. God was so gracious, He had blessed my obedience in walking on to the site, despite my fear, and used that one act to begin an outpouring of love among the gypsies.

I went back to the site every day for the next three weeks and fifteen people got converted, including the man and his wife, and another fifteen were baptised.

At this very beginning of my ministry to the gypsies, the Lord said to me in a verse from John 15 v 16, '*You have not chosen me, but I have chosen you, and ordained you that you shall bring forth fruit, and your fruit shall remain.*' In these words He gently told me that the fruits of my ministry would be permanent, and not fade away. In this respect I've been very, very fortunate, because I've seen the lasting fruit of my labours, when many people don't.

When I first started preaching, drugs weren't even heard of, but now they're everywhere. The gypsies tended to drink – although only a minority were excessive drinkers - but their culture is violent, and fights often break out. They have terrible feuds, and can kill each other - I personally knew six men killed by violent gypsies. But they don't fight outsiders. Their culture is very hierarchical and matriarchal. They live in complete family communities, and the mother is in charge. These were Romany people who had no time at all for the modern travellers.

They love fortune-telling but I stopped them doing it. All the older women would try and cross my palm with silver, and give me a gypsy blessing. When they take against a person they 'beg a prayer' on them and pray harm will come to them. These gypsy curses are powerful and the power may be real, but we can always overcome the Devil by the blood of the lamb. The gypsies obey me, normally speaking, and say now as they did from the early days, 'If the Pastor says don't do something, don't do it.'

The gypsies in Kent have experienced God's power first-hand. Although I've never been tempted in the direction of the occult, thank the Lord, I understand the spiritual vacuum in the modern world. Nature abhors a vacuum, and that's true spiritually, so if a person isn't filled by the Lord, they can be filled by the Devil. That's what happens.

Jesus did say there will be more in hell than heaven, *'Narrow is the way that leads to heaven and few there be that go thereby, wide is the road that leads to Hell and many of the weak shall go that way.'*[23]

In the middle of winter in the late 1960's, snow was falling and had settled on the ground while I was preaching with Fred on a gypsy site. The gypsies suggested we stayed with them, as my home was sixty miles away. I was tempted to accept and go home next day, but the Lord made it very clear that he wanted me to leave.

We began walking down the track and as we started out, I saw the headlights of a car coming down the road. I put my hand up and the car stopped. As the passenger door opened, I saw a Bible on the seat. The driver turned out to be a born again solicitor but he said, 'I can't take you far because I'm very late.'

I said, 'That's fine'.

After he dropped us we found ourselves in a wood with no houses anywhere, nothing. We walked down the road until I heard a car coming and as it drew level, I called, 'Could you give us a lift?'

'Yes.'

Then I realised the car was full of teddy boys, with

shaven heads, rings in their ears and rings in their noses. I thought, 'Oh dear, oh dear! And I've got to tell them I'm a Christian.'

I thanked them very much and said, 'Actually I'm a Christian minister of God and just trust God and pray for lifts.'

There was a deathly silence and I wondered what on earth they were going to do or say.

One of them blurted out in a really rough voice, 'I got saved last night.'

'What do you mean? Tell me.'

'I took Jesus into my life, I was born again.'

The three teddy boys had been converted the night before. So we pulled in at the side of the road and I ministered to them for over an hour, then they drove us home. That was a wonderful work of God's sovereignty to bring us together like that, just when they needed the spiritual food I was able to give them.

Another night, after I'd been preaching all day on a gypsy site called Cox's Lane near Epsom, it was late and again the gypsies asked me to stay.

I said, 'No Charlie, I've got faith to believe that through the dark of a winter's night God is sending me a lift to take me straight home.' I said that in complete faith.

'At least let me run you down to the roundabout.'

So he drove me two miles and dropped me off. There was no traffic and it was very cold, but I had faith and believed. A man *was* sent by God, in the first car that came by. The driver said 'I'm only going three miles down the road,' and I thought three miles was better than nothing, got in, thanked him and told him about my faith.

'Where are you going?'

'Tunbridge Wells.'

'Well I'll drive you there, if the next garage is open.' It was, and the driver filled up and drove the round trip of 120 miles.

I was amazed and told him he was very good.

He said, 'It isn't good of me – I wanted to meet a man who knows God like you do.'

He took me all the way to my house. He was a deep-sea diver and said he wanted to find God. I explained how he could.

Whatever a man says in faith will happen, and I believed the Lord would send me the right lifts.

After I'd been preaching to some gypsies at Hosey Common in a caravan, it got late and a gypsy called Jasper asked how I would get home, 'All the buses have gone and you haven't got a car.'

I told him I had faith that God would get me home. As I said these words there was a knock on the caravan door and two drunks came in to see Jasper. They weren't gypsies.

'Who's this?' one said, pointing at me.

'He's a minister of God.'

'I don't believe in all that nonsense,' he replied.

'Well this man's got enough faith to believe somebody's going to come through the dark and take him home.'

'Don't you believe a word he says – he'll have a car parked round the corner to take him home.'

I butted in, 'I have not. So you don't believe in God then? Can I ask who you think put the moon and the stars up there?'

And we talked for over a couple of hours until he'd sobered up and gradually in the end he started to listen to what I was saying.

At last he said, 'I'll tell you what I believe - that you're an honest man. I'll drive you home.'

When we set off he said, 'How about coming to have a meal with me?'

It was one in the morning. We had a lovely meal of bacon and eggs, and then he drove me home.

The word I spoke to him was this, 'Salvation is like a bridge across a river. It's there for everybody to cross if they want to, and it's the only way across the river. If you choose not to use the bridge, you won't get to the other side. That's exactly like the Gospel – Jesus died for all our sins but the cross will only save you if you believe in it.'

That man was really struck by the words, and drove me all the way to my door.

I was preaching in Horsmonden one summer's day when a gypsy pulled up in his lorry and began chatting. After a while he asked, 'Where did you park your car?'

'I haven't got one.'

He offered to take me to Tunbridge Wells, but soon after we set off, his car ran out of petrol and we were stuck at the side of the road.

Bill said, 'I'm going to see if I can find a piece of rubber tubing.'

I knew what he was going to do, steal petrol by siphoning it from somebody else's tank into a container. Off he went and I prayed with my eyes closed and asked the Lord to show us what to do and send us petrol.

When I opened my eyes there was a man standing pouring petrol out of a can into our tank. I couldn't believe my eyes and said, 'I'm afraid I haven't got any money.'

'That's all right,' he said, and carried on pouring.

'You're very kind. How did you know I needed petrol?'

'I just thought you might need some, so I put it in.' And away he went. What a wonderful answer to prayer!

Bill came back and said, 'No luck.'

I said, 'Just turn the ignition key.'

The engine went tick, tick as it sucked up the petrol and started.

Bill said, 'Wherever did you get that from?' And I told him.

That's the way God witnessed to gypsies.

In 1965, six years after forming the church at Goudhurst, I met a brother in the Lord in Tunbridge Wells while I was walking.

'How are you John?' he called.

'Very well, the Lord's doing such wonderful things here in our little churches.'

'Praise the Lord! But how do you manage without a car?'

I simply trust God to provide a lift.'

'But if you had a car, you'd have more time on your hands. Look John, I've just bought a new car and don't know what to do with my old one, so I'd like to give it to you for your work.'

'That's very generous, but could you give me a couple of days to pray about it?' I asked him, aware how much I was being blessed by the walking and meeting many people through it. Eventually I accepted the car for six months until it petered out, and after that I was offered the first of a series of 12-seater minibuses for the use of the church. We've run six buses since 1965, and they've been marvellous for bringing folk to services who have no other means of transport.

Ever since I'd begun to live by faith and given everything away, my mother wouldn't have me in her house. When I got converted she stopped speaking to me, apart from saying, 'You've got no right to be preaching John, you haven't been to theological college and you're not ordained. I won't listen to a word you've got to say.'

Fights like this happen in families when people are saved, it's the Devil. Jesus said, '*I came not to bring peace but a sword, a mother-in-law against a daughter-in-law, a son against his father.'*[24] That's why I'm always very careful what I pray for - humans we may want a happy family, but God wants a saved family.

I prayed for my mother every day for seventeen years, never missed, until 1970 when she became very ill and went into a hospice.

The matron told me mother wouldn't last much longer, a day or two at the very most. And I thought – she's not saved! Then she passed into unconsciousness and I couldn't get to her.

I went to Fred Scruton and said, 'Look Fred, my mother's dying. She's only got a few hours to live and she's not saved. We've got to pray. Do you agree you want my mother back to consciousness and saved?' He said, 'I agree.' And we prayed.

I'd learned the power of that verse a few years earlier when Fred and I were stranded in the pouring rain at night in the middle of winter. We were drenched and no cars would stop for us. I'd said, 'Come on Fred, we've got to agree.' We turned our backs to the road under the cover of a tree and I prayed, '*Again I say unto you, if two of you on earth shall agree, anything they ask, it shall be done for you by your Father in heaven,*'[25] and as I prayed a car stopped. I've used that verse thousands of times, and know the power of it.

After praying, I returned to the hospice and found my mother sitting up in bed drinking a cup of tea.

I said, 'Mother, it's time to take Jesus into your heart as your Saviour.'

For the first time in my life I heard her say, 'You're right John, I should.' She took Jesus as her Saviour and two hours later the Lord took her. It was God's grace, because Fred and I had both agreed, using the power of that verse from Scripture.

So after seventeen years of daily prayer, my mother

was saved. Alleluia!

A gypsy family asked me to minister to a man of about 60 who was in the last stages of cancer of the throat. His relations were regular attendees at church and wanted him to be baptised before he died, and I arranged to baptise him three weeks later. But his health deteriorated so badly, that when he arrived for baptism on that Sunday morning, he had to be supported by his two sons and could barely talk or breathe.

I thought – heck, if I baptise that man, he'll die and they will all blame me. That's what the Devil said to me, because gypsies are very funny about death.

So I went over before the service and whispered, 'Look my old friend, I can see you're not well enough to be baptised today, don't you think we ought to put it off until you're a bit better?'

The poor man mouthed his reply through dry lips, 'This is my only chance. Please!'

I closed my eyes and prayed desperately, 'Lord I'm going to trust you and baptise him.'

So we held the service and I baptised the frail, sick man by full immersion, and as I lifted him out of the water he looked utterly different. I hardly believed it then, but we later had medical confirmation that he'd been fully and completely healed from his cancer. There was no longer anything there.

He went under the water with cancer, and came up healed. For a long while afterwards I thought to myself – and I nearly didn't baptise him – shame on me! And I vowed never to listen to the voice of the Devil telling me not to trust God, whose own word tells us to claim His power to *'cleanse the lepers, and raise the dead.'* [26] Who are we to question that word, which I know is as relevant and powerful today as it was two thousand years ago?

On one of my first visits to the gypsies a woman

approached me and asked me to pray for her son Bill who was in terrible pain. I went into her caravan which was full of children, and saw their father lying in intense pain on the bed.

The woman told me he and another man had been trying to lift a lorry engine which had slipped, and fallen on to his leg, breaking it. The Kent & Sussex Hospital had put the leg in plaster.

I asked him, 'Are you in great pain?'

'Terrible pain. They've put my leg in plaster, but I have to go back to have it re-broken and re-set. The pain's terrible.'

'I'll pray for you, just close your eyes.'

He did, and all the children did, and I laid hands on him and felt the familiar healing power of Jesus come right through me and into him.

When he opened his eyes he said, 'Thank God for that - the pain's gone.'

Later he returned to hospital to have his leg reset, but when he told the doctor all the pain had gone, they took another X-ray. When they examined it they found the break in the bone was completely healed. Praise the Lord!

Of course the story of that healing spread through the gypsy network like wildfire, and early one morning soon afterwards I heard the Lord say to me, 'You're going to stand in front of the highest in the land.'

It wasn't long before that word came true, as I began to speak for gypsies in court.

It hadn't taken me long to work out that in general, the gypsies didn't believe in God and didn't even believe each other. They told so many lies that there was very little trust between them. When I first got involved in helping them, they would check up on me because they wouldn't trust me either.

That happened after I'd agreed to go and pray for a

gypsy child who was critically ill in Great Ormond Street Hospital. I'd promised the parents I would go.

When I arrived, a nurse asked me to wait in a side room while she made arrangements to see the child, and I waited. The room had a telephone in it.

Suddenly the phone rang, and I picked it up. I was stunned to hear the child's father on the line, checking up on me. So he had proof that I was there – I'd actually answered the phone! So, little by little the gypsies came to trust me.

Time and time again, they came to me and said, 'Pastor I've got into a spot of trouble, can you help me?'

I always said, 'Yes, but you've got to be completely honest with me so I can help.' But they never were. It was only when I reached court that I had the full picture. Then I had it in glorious colour! After a while I stopped making assumptions, and just spoke up for gypsies with facts that would help them, saying, 'Just because I'm here speaking for this man doesn't mean I agree with him, but I can say this - he's a good father and a good husband.'

Just being there made a difference to the outcome, I always felt Judges would avoid giving a prison sentence if they could, and when they saw a defendant had somebody trustworthy who would help their rehabilitation, they chose that option instead of prison.

At this point John produced a bundle of old newspaper clippings from a drawer. After only a few minutes in his room it was obvious to me that he owns almost nothing. The pictures and furniture in his room at Cornford House are not his own, and that's why he had remarked about the photo of himself with the DFC. It was not usual for him to keep things. Apart from that picture, and a couple of snaps of gypsies at Goudhurst church, he has nothing, and the Bible is the only book he has read since 1960. But he's kept a few press clippings of his court appearances, which I have placed in chronological order here.

February 1970
A 53 year old labourer with 17 previous convictions was ready for rehabilitation, Pastor Lywood told the East Sussex sessions at Lewes. Frederick Elkington admitted burglariously entering a home at Cross-in-hand and stealing property worth £21 8s 4d. The court heard that he got into the house by removing an extractor fan. He spent the night there having something to eat and drink and playing records. The owners were away. Pastor Lywood said he had spent much time in the past 11 years trying to assist down and out people. He had helped to rehabilitate about 12 people and he thought Elkington needed this kind of help. He had known him for 3 years. Elkington was put on probation for 3 years. The chairman asked the probation service to do all it could to help his rehabilitation.

24 November 1972 Courier
It takes a lot to bring a busy Kent gypsy camp to a standstill. But when Pastor Lywood arrives, families crowd round to greet him. The gypsies of Kent - normally suspicious of outsiders - have put their trust in him. He travels thousands of miles in his well-worn minibus visiting camps throughout the county each year, and he can safely chat with the roughest gypsy, even in the most hostile camps. From his tiny one-room home in Tunbridge Wells he works a huge parish and has taken under his wing some of the most intractable parishioners around - down and outs, tramps, and the strongly independent gypsies.

It has taken Mr Lywood years of often heart-breaking work to win their confidence.

20 years ago, Mr Lywood was happy to proclaim himself an atheist. Christianity was just a word, he never went to church and he was not interested in the work of the church.

'I started to have remarkable religious experiences, and I became conscious that there was a God. To face up to the

implications of believing took a long time. Instead of going to race meetings, I started going to church. Instead of trying to get people into pubs, I started trying to get them out.'

A number of people have preached to gypsies in their own camps, but Mr Lywood is one of the few who have succeeded in persuading them to go to church on Sunday. The rest of his week is taken up with visiting prisons all over Kent, helping the gypsies in trouble with the law, teaching them to drive, and persuading them to tax their cars.

He also campaigns against their habit of dumping old cars on roadsides, 'I told them that leaving this rubbish all over the countryside was one of the things that made them unpopular. These gypsies are definitely a race apart. They are so often misunderstood and the awful part of the problem is that they have nowhere to go.'

I'd got to know a gypsy woman whose husband I'd never met but who had a terrible record. He was in youth custody by age twelve, and by forty he'd never had more than three months free, it was a ghastly record. During a burglary he was caught, hit a policeman and hospitalised him. He was known as Jukebox Johnnie Smith.

I said to his wife, 'Lena, tell John if he wants me to, I'll speak for him in court.'

'It won't be necessary Pastor, we've got a very good barrister already.'

As soon as she said that, I knew in my heart that they'd had it, and sure enough, her husband got four and a half years. So Lena asked me to drive her to visit John in Wormwood scrubs, and that's how I came to know this very, very tough man.

After about six months I asked him, 'Now John, why don't you appeal?'

'No,' he said, 'I'm guilty and I've got to do the time.'

'John, I think you should appeal.'

'Well if you want to, go ahead,' he said.

So I put the appeal through, and eventually it came to the High Court, at the Royal Courts of Justice. I prayed very, very deeply that I would help him out of prison, and felt God say I would be able to drive him home the same day.

In court John's barrister said, 'Pastor Lywood - it's very kind of you to come all the way to London to speak for this man, but I'm very sorry, only a barrister is allowed to speak in the high court. But you're very welcome to sit at the back and listen.'

So I sat at the back and the barrister spoke for John.

After about half an hour, the three Lords Justice said to the barrister, 'We've heard enough. Smith stand up.'

John stood, handcuffed to a warder.

'Smith, you've got a terrible record of robbery, violence and deceit, you've hardly had any freedom in your life, and we don't think we should reduce your sentence, but increase it by a couple of years. Take him away!' And away he went.

I prayed desperately, 'Lord - you said I was going to drive him home!'

As I prayed that prayer, the barrister who'd said I couldn't speak, stood up and announced, 'Excuse me my Lord, there's a minister here who knows John.'

As soon as I heard that, I walked forward.

The Lord Chief Justice said, 'Do you know that man who's just walked out?'

'Yes I know him very well indeed.'

'Who are you?'

'I'm a minister, pastor of the church.' And I told him all the good things I could think of, and promised to keep an eye on John.

The Judges went out and came back in again and asked the warder to fetch John back. (The barrister told me afterwards this wasn't correct procedure.)

He stood in handcuffs and the Lord Chief Justice said, 'Smith, we said you couldn't have your freedom, but that was before we heard Pastor Lywood speak. The Judge and jury that gave you the four and a half years never heard Pastor Lywood speak either. We have. So we're going to take a very unusual step, and let you go.'

The warder took off the handcuffs and I drove him home thinking 'No-one's going to believe this!'

A fortnight later, I was in a gypsy site just north of London and a woman I'd never seen before in my life came up and said, 'Cor - you did well for Johnnie Smith!'

'What do you mean?'

'Well it's all in the Comet.'

'What do you mean, the comic?'

'No, the paper, the Comet.'

I got hold of the newspaper and found the headline, PLEA BY A CLERGYMAN.

4 April 1973, Surrey Comet

A gypsy said by a High Court Judge to have had 'very little freedom in the last 12 years' was freed from a four and a half year jail sentence on Monday.

John Smith 38, landscape gardener of Epsom, was jailed by Surbiton crown court last July for burglary and assaulting police.

The appeal court judge said there was 'no substance in his application' for assaulting police to be quashed.

'Assaults on officers in the execution of their duty are grave offences, when committed by a man who has previously received a custodial sentence for the same thing, some 3 years previously. Bearing in mind the shocking record of this man, with no less than 14 previous offences, it is not surprising that he was sentenced to a substantial term of imprisonment,' said the Judge.

'But the court has had the special advantage of hearing Rev Lywood give evidence on behalf of this man. Lywood has told the court he had known Smith for 5 years, and the woman he had recently married for 10. He feels confident that if this man is given a truly extraordinary chance by this court, there is a chance that he will take it and keep out of trouble in future. This court proposes to take the wholly exceptional course of substituting an order that the sentences shall run concurrently and shall be of such length that he can be freed from custody tomorrow.'

This report is accurate except John actually came out the same day and I took him home. And he's never been in trouble since - that decision stopped him from offending again. I knew this was the wonderful proof the gypsies needed of God's power. I should never have been speaking in the High Court, and had no legal training. It was wonderful.

The Bible tells us God has great love and compassion for those in prison. I was supporting a young gypsy lad who was in the police cells attached to the magistrates' court. His barrister invited me to come down to the cell where she was going to speak to the boy. The warder opened a door with keys, clanged it behind us, then opened another barred door until we reached the lad.

He was in a terrible cell with no fresh air and no window, cooped up like a wild animal. I felt such compassion for that young man sweep over me from the Lord that it touched the barrister and she immediately turned to me and said, 'Do you enjoy your work? Where does this wonderful compassion come from?'

We had a long talk and she said, 'My father was a priest and left the Catholic church to marry my mother. I don't think he's ever got over it.'

We had a deep discussion about salvation, and I feel

much fruit came from that. The love of the Holy Spirit which swept through me on to that young man had touched her, and she had felt it.

24 May 1974, Kent Messenger

Armed with a Bible, and his own courage, Pastor Lywood strode into a large gypsy encampment near Goudhurst. He was a complete stranger to the nomadic residents.

Pastor Lywood, a slightly built and softly spoken man, has earned the respect and friendship of more than 3,000 gypsies who he now thinks live in this county. They come in their hundreds to his church for services on a Sunday. Over the years Pastor Lywood has built up a true understanding of Kent's illiterate and homeless peoples.

He often appears in court cases and speaks on a gypsy's behalf. His word is respected.

His life today, driving round the Kent countryside in a battered pea-green Dormobile, calling on the gypsy families, preaching to them and ferrying them all over the country in his easily recognisable van, is a far cry from his former life.

As I ministered to the gypsies, the Holy Spirit revealed to them not to do wrong. Many times I read them a verse from Ephesians, *'Let him that stole steal no more, but rather let him labour, working with his hands that he may give to him that needs.'* [27]

One night I read that verse to a gypsy, and three months later he and two others were on their way to break into a house. As he was driving along those words came back to him.

He suddenly said, 'Let me out.'

'What do you mean?'

'Just stop the car and let me out.'

The two other gypsies went on without him, did the burglary, were caught and served two years in prison, but this man was free.

He told so many gypsies that it was a powerful witness.

From the very start I never condoned wrong-doing, but I've seen people change dramatically - there's absolutely no question about it.

A Judge said to me in court once, 'Pastor Lywood, I need to say something, I sit here day after day, week after week, and year after year, and everyone who comes in front of me is a villain. They're all villains, all tarred with the same brush, and not one of them alters.'

I replied, 'Excuse me Your Honour, I know one that did alter.' And I told him about Jukebox Johnnie Smith.

'So they do change?' he said.

God really used my background and education, because I came from the same social level as judges, but it was the power of His Spirit that turned their hearts around, without their knowing it, towards the Lord and towards the people I was speaking for.

I remember one very hard, tough gypsy who'd been in prison many times, and through one winter I led him to the Lord. One night as we stood round the gypsy camp fire, without a single word he put his hand in his pocket, took out a pack of cards and threw it on the fire, 'I'll never gamble again,' he said.

The gypsies truly changed after they were saved. The Bible says, *'By their fruits you shall know them'*.[28] The change was entirely the Lord's doing, I couldn't do it. Give God the glory. None of this is about me, it's about what the Lord has done through me.

People have always asked me questions and I haven't got the answers, although God has given me words of wisdom at certain times. One day in a crown court I was speaking for four gypsies who were real cowboys, knocking on doors and doing work worth £10 and charging £1,000. The court was absolutely packed, and I was called forward.

The Judge said, 'Pastor Lywood, don't you think you'd be far better employed looking after the poor victims who've had their money taken, instead of these villains?'

I thought – what on earth am I going to say to that?

Straight away the Lord gave me the word, 'You're right Your Honour, I do believe that, but the victims are not on trial, these four men are.'

That was the wisdom of Solomon, and there was no answer the Judge could give. Those weren't my words, they were the Lord's.

I have supported people who were in the wrong, but I reach out with God's love and show them the proof that although they've done wrong and must be punished, God has not turned away from them. That's the message I bring.

Greater things than this you shall see

By the early 1970s the congregation in our little church in Goudhurst was a motley crew of gypsies, tramps, ex-prisoners and some locals. The congregation stayed all day. Services began at 11a.m. with worship and praise, followed by a buffet lunch. A thriving 3 p.m. Sunday school was run by Erica Charrington who drove the minibus, and collected children from surrounding villages. Evening service began at 6.15p.m.

As the teaching and preaching of the Gospel spread throughout the gypsies in Kent, hundreds got converted and baptised and many signs and wonders and healings were wrought in their midst.

One day I was preaching and ministering to gypsies in the hop fields when I was asked to pray by a young girl who was very worried about her sister's forthcoming serious operation.

The girl said, 'I've put my faith and trust in Jesus,' and pulled a crucifix out of her clothing.

A gypsy called Caroline butted in, 'Jesus isn't there, he's up there,' and pointed to heaven.

I was amazed to hear those words and said to the girl, 'If you want your sister to be healed, what you need to do is go home, get rid of that crucifix, and let Jesus come into your heart, then pray for your sister.'

'Oh I could never do that, I can't part from this,' she said, clutching the crucifix closer.

Four days later I was in the same hop field when the girl came running to me saying, 'I did it, did what you said - threw the crucifix away and asked Jesus to come into my heart. And you know what - he did! My sister's recovered and doesn't need the operation.' Glory be to God.

As I was driving through Tunbridge Wells, the sister of a woman named Patience Harris from our congregation was on the pavement and flagged me down saying, 'Patience has fallen out of a tree, broken her pelvis and she's in Kent & Sussex Hospital.'

When I arrived, the staff nurse told me, 'Patience is very bad, she's broken her pelvis in two places and she must lie on her back without moving for six weeks.'

It was true - she was in terrible pain. If she moved even her toe it was excruciating.

She told me, 'As I fell out of the tree I asked God to save me. When I hit the ground everybody thought I was dead. I know God spared my life, and I've got enough faith to believe that if you pray for me now, I'll be healed.'

I sensed the depth of her faith, and when I laid hands on her, I felt that healing power come down through me on to her. When I finished she was covered with sweat from the top of her head to the soles of her feet, she was burning hot.

'All the pain's gone!' she said.

I said 'Try and move your toe.'

'There's no pain!'

She moved her foot, her leg, and then got out of bed. There was no pain. I told her to climb back into bed and I left.

A few days later I found her hospital bed empty. The woman in the next bed said, 'Patience went home a couple of days ago.'

So I found a nurse who said, 'Are you the man who prayed for her? The whole hospital's talking about this, she's completely healed, it's wonderful. We can't get over it, will you come in and tell us how you did it?' So I witnessed to her and another nurse about the healing power of Jesus.

The nurse said that after I'd left, Patience had insisted

she was healed, but the staff nurse wouldn't believe her. Patience insisted she saw a doctor and eventually, rather reluctantly, a doctor examined her and said, 'It certainly does feel as if she's healed, but we need an X-ray.'

The X-ray showed she was completely healed. To God be the glory.

Many times I went to visit a sick person in hospital and a doctor would say, 'I'm very sorry, there's nothing we can do, they might last an hour.'

I would lay hands on them, and God rose them up nearly every time. The doctors would say, 'Well these things sometimes happen,' or any old excuse - they would never agree a miracle had taken place.

I have a photo of a woman called Elsie Kent, and one night at midnight I had a call saying she'd had a stroke, and wasn't expected to live. I threw on my clothes and went straight to the hospital.

The staff nurse said, 'You'd better be quick because Elsie's kidneys have packed up and the doctors reckon she has fifteen minutes to live. If you want to see her alive you'll have to go in now.'

I knelt down to commit her soul to the Lord, but He said to me, 'Stand up, lay your hands on her and I'll raise her up.' So I stood, laid my hands on her and she came out of her crisis, and lived for five years.

Every time the Lord has promised to heal someone, He's done it. Wonderful, incredible. Jesus said *'Greater things than this you shall see'* [29] but we haven't got enough faith. *'The prayers of the faithful save the sick....Whatever a man says in faith will happen.'* [30]

The Lord did greatly bless my healing ministry, and there have been so many miracles! One brilliant summer day a gypsy I knew was driving his lorry along the bypass near Sevenoaks with his nephew Freddie who was fourteen. Suddenly the lorry broke down, and they pulled in at the side of the road and went under the lorry to diagnose the problem. But an articulated lorry driving at 70 miles an hour went slap into the back of their vehicle, pushing it over the two bodies. When they were pulled out, the paramedics thought they were both dead.

Only a fortnight earlier I had been standing round the camp fire with the man, and after everyone else went to bed he'd said, 'Do you know what Pastor? I want the Lord to take me.'

'You shouldn't say things like that, you're only forty, perfectly healthy, with plenty of money and a lovely wife and children.'

'Yeah but I'm fed up, I get up in the morning, go to work, go to bed, and get up again. I want the Lord to take me.'

He died on the way to hospital, although his young nephew was just living. That made me realise how careful we should be about what we say, or pray for.

As soon as I heard about the accident, I went straight to the hospital, and asked the doctor if the boy would live.

'No he won't, and it's far better if he doesn't, because he would only be a cabbage. The wheel of the lorry has gone over his pelvis and smashed it into a hundred pieces, smithereens. There's no way it can ever be mended.'

'Can I see him?'

'He's unconscious, but if you want to, yes.'

As I went into the room, Freddie opened his eyes and recognised me. I saw his lips move and bent right down to put my ear next to his mouth. He whispered, 'Ask Jesus to take away the pain.'

I thought - that boy's got faith, he hasn't asked for a doctor, or painkillers, he's asked for Jesus. So I laid hands on him and prayed in faith, and felt the healing power go down into his body.

Five days later I went back to the hospital and bumped right into the doctor.

'You're just the man I'm looking for,' he said, 'Come into my office and sit down'.

I honestly thought he was going to tell me Freddie was dead. But instead he said, 'Wonders will never cease. You know that boy you prayed for, every bit of bone, every bit of muscle, vein and tissue has gone back into place.'

Later on, the X-rays were shown to a Harley Street orthopaedic consultant, one of the most senior in Britain, who then asked to see me and Freddie. He held up the X-ray taken immediately after the accident and said, 'There's no way anybody with injuries like this could ever walk again.' Then he said to Freddie 'Hop across the floor on one leg,' and he did.

Then he held up the X-ray taken after I had prayed for healing, 'Now hop across the floor on the other leg.' And Freddie did.

The consultant threw the X-rays down and said to me, 'If ever I've seen a miracle that's it. How did you do it?'

'I'm a minister of God, and laid hands on him and prayed. Jesus has healed him.'

'That's a miracle!'

'Well, God did it.'

But then, like so many of the doctors who have seen evidence of healings, he tried to laugh it off, 'I tell you what, you come up to Harley Street and work with me, and the ones I can't heal, you can do!' He was only mocking, but we give God the glory, that Freddie is now a grown man, married with two children, and bones as sound as anyone. Praise the Lord!'

There's a story in the Bible about Philip and the Eunuch, where the Lord lifted Philip up and hid him from sight.[31] The Lord once kept me hidden like that for three weeks. One day during the hop-picking season while the men were at work, I went to preach to the families who were left behind in the caravans. As I arrived at the farm, the young son of the farmer shouted, 'Oi you - out! We don't want you here or anybody like you. Get off my premises and don't come back on my land again.' He was a very arrogant and proud young man.

So I left. But the next day the Lord said to me, 'Go back to that farm again and I will hide you.'

For three weeks I went to that farm every single day and was hidden. The farmer's son saw me but God hid me from his eyes. I was within his vision but he never saw me. On the last Saturday I walked in through the gate and he was driving towards me up the drive, in his Landrover. I thought - He's got to see me now, he's driving right past me! But God hid me.

He'd just got married and two days after shouting at me I read in the paper that all his wedding presents had been stolen from his house. I know God punishes people, as written in Hebrews – '*Whom the Lord loves he chastens, he scourges every son that he receives.*' [32] To this day, whenever I walk through Goudhurst and that farmer passes in his jeep, he lowers his eyes in shame, and can't look me in the face.

The Methodist minister once invited me to come to speak to his youth group and I agreed. That evening about twenty teenagers turned up and I preached the Gospel and gave them the opportunity to make a commitment if anybody wanted to take Jesus into their heart as Saviour.

I said, 'If any of you want to take Jesus into your heart and be born again, I'll be in that little room, just come in and I'll be there.'

Three or four youngsters came to me and made commitments. To each I asked the same simple questions,

'Do you love and accept Jesus into your life?' The next person to come in was a girl whose father I knew as a very rich farmer in Goudhurst. I began to ask her the same questions as the others, but her response shocked me.

'Who the hell do you think you are?' she shouted, 'asking me questions like that. It's none of your business what I think.' And with that she flounced out of the room.

The very next day I had a phone call from her father who was absolutely furious.

'What do you mean by speaking to my daughter like that? You should mind your own business - she came home very upset indeed,' and he went on getting angrier and louder for several minutes.

'You're an idiot and your God's an idiot, the whole business stinks and we don't want the likes of you round here,' and he began to run God down more viciously. But I was amazed to find that the more he said, and the worse his language became, I felt more love for him. The love can only have come from God, because in the past I would have shouted back. The father slammed the phone down, and I still felt such love for him.

Three days later the Methodist minister rushed into our church at Goudhurst in a fluster, 'Have you heard? The day after our youth meeting, that rich farmer who was so angry with you just dropped down dead where he stood. There wasn't anything wrong with him until then!'

I stared at my friend in disbelief. Into my head came the words, *'God is the same yesterday, today and for ever. He is a holy God.'*[33] That incident proved that God sometimes shows us people can't trifle with Christians and his ministers, He defends those who love Him.

My first experience of this power had happened in 1954 when I first got converted. I'd known a schoolmaster who was a great name-dropper and gravitated towards the wealthy aristocracy. We'd met at the Brenchley Amateur Dramatic Society and he thought I was the cat's whiskers because I was young and rich. But after my conversion he wouldn't speak to me. We met by chance in the Brenchley village hall, and I could tell he despised me because I was no longer rich.

Vowing to be kind and loving I said, 'How are you?'

He puffed himself up and looked at me as if I were a piece of dirt and said 'I'm all right.' As if to say – 'Look at me. How about you? I don't need God - look at me, I'm all right and you're not.' Then he mocked me about walking the roads and begging for money.

At five o'clock that evening he dropped down dead, although he had been in perfect health. The barman had witnessed the way he spoke to me and was amazed, he recognised this as a warning to us never to set ourselves up against God.

If we trust God in faith he will answer our every need and rescue us from every predicament. I was driving members of our congregation home on the minibus one bitterly cold winter's evening when the van broke down.

We tried everything we could to no avail and I prayed, 'Heavenly Father, you said you would never leave me or forsake me. What can I do about all these people?'

The Lord said, 'Trust me, do what you always do, pray.' So I prayed someone would stop and help. Immediately a driver stopped and asked, 'Are you in trouble?'

'Yes, we were driving home from our last service and the minibus has broken down. You're not going into Tunbridge Wells by any chance are you?'

'Yes we are.'

'Would you mind taking this disabled lady home?'

'Certainly, no trouble.'

We got her in and away she went. Then I prayed nine

more times, and nine cars stopped until the last person in the minibus had been taken home. Then I was alone by the side of the minibus and thought, 'There's no-one with me, what can I do?'

The Lord clearly told me, 'Get a lift to the gypsy site in Stybridge and John King will help you.'

As I arrived on the site I saw John silhouetted in the light from his caravan, as if he was waiting for me. I said, 'I got lifts John - the minibus has broken down.'

He drove me home to Tunbridge Wells, went back to the minibus and towed that back to Maidstone. Next day I got lifts by faith to the gypsy site and lo and behold! They'd mended the bus and it was running perfectly. Glory be to God.

God always protects and looks after his children, for example when I was driving down the M1 from Leeds to London doing 70mph in the fast lane. Suddenly the Lord said to me, 'Pull into the slow lane and reduce your speed to 30mph.'

I pulled over, reduced my speed and as I reached 30mph, a tyre burst.

We had a midweek service in Brenchley every Wednesday and I used to pick up children in the bus. One week I drove down the steep hill to pick up Caroline, her children and grand-children in the minibus. We were having engine trouble, and I realised we'd never get up the hill with a full load, so I said, 'You'll have to get out at the bottom of the hill and walk with the children because the bus won't make it.'

Caroline said, 'Trust the Lord,' and as she said it, power went into the accelerator and we shot up the hill. Next day I drove to the garage and when the mechanic looked at the bus he said, 'Who towed you up here this morning?'

'Nobody, I drove.'

'Your valves are completely burned out – this bus couldn't be driven.'

'If I told you yesterday we went up a steep hill with a full load would you believe me?'

'That's completely impossible.'

One Sunday a regular worshipper forgot to switch her headlights off when she arrived at church in the mist. When she tried to start her car, the battery was flat. Three of us pushed the car down the hill in Goudhurst to bump start it, but at the bottom the engine hadn't responded and I thought, 'We're at the bottom, nothing's going to make this car start.'

Then I said to the others, 'Jesus raised Lazarus from the dead so let's ask Him to put that power into this battery. Close your eyes and I'll pray.' I prayed in Jesus' name, laid hands on the car, and immediately the lights came on and the engine started. That was a real Holy Spirit miracle.

The Bible says the Lord will always confirm the word of his servant,[34] and once I preached to a gypsy family about how Jesus was betrayed by Judas Iscariot. The next morning when I walked down to the gypsy camp, those very verses of scripture were being preached over national radio as I arrived.

On one occasion I preached to gypsies on the text, *'Behold I stand at the door and knock, and if any man hears and opens the door I will come in,'*[35] and I held up the picture by William Holman Hunt depicting Jesus as the light of the world. About ten days later I was standing around a gypsy fire preaching to a dozen men who were seated on the ground listening to me. One said, 'I've got something to tell you Pastor. I was driving along the other day, saw a shed and wondered what was in it.'

Gypsies often trespass, so I wasn't surprised.

'I opened the door and there was nothing inside

except a pile of rubbish, but as I turned to leave I saw a small white piece of card at the edge of the heap and pulled it out. I could see it was a painting, and it turned out to be a large copy of that picture of Jesus knocking on the door you showed us a few days ago.'

During another time of preaching on the edge of a hop field, a very strong wind blew up while I was telling them of Jesus going to sleep in the boat when the wind and waves got up. In the story the apostles thought they would drown and they woke Jesus. He stood, put up His hands and commanded the wind and the waves, 'Peace - be still!'[36] The moment I said those words, the wind in the hop field stopped and there was a great calm. Incidents like that were such a powerful witness.

5 April 1978

A self-employed roofer has been freed from jail thanks to a visiting priest. Pastor Lywood told 3 appeal court Judges that he has visited David Thursting who comes from Wimbledon in prison. 'I am not I hope a gullible man, I was very impressed by his very real desire for reformation.' Thursting was jailed last September for 15 months for deception. The appeal court substituted a sentence that enabled his immediate release. The Appeal Judge said Thursting's record was appalling but the court was impressed by Mr Lywood's assessment of Thursting and that he had reached the turning point of his life.

1980 Kent Messenger

Pastor Lywood spoke out against the harassment of gypsies, and represented two brothers at a planning enquiry in Maidstone after they had been refused planning permission for their caravans. He said, 'Gypsies have been pilloried and harassed for 100 years.' The brothers, who are members of Goudhurst church, have saved the money to buy their own land.

1986 Kent Messenger

A clergyman told a court why he did not think a gypsy woman caught shoplifting would offend again. Mr Lywood said Adams attended his church and was a good wife and mother. He had been perplexed as to why she had committed the offences until he discovered her husband had left her after an argument.

Failure by local authorities to carry out their duty to provide gypsy sites was attacked by Pastor Lywood at court last week. He was speaking on behalf of Jack Newland, a Romany, who denied breaking a district council order by living with his wife and 3 children in a bungalow converted from 2 mobile caravan units. The council enforcement notice was served on the previous owner of the site. Newland told the magistrate he had 'a little idea' about the notice when he bought the land. 'My wife and I cannot read and are not experienced in legal matters and the previous owner could not read either.' He produced receipts showing he had paid the rates on his unauthorised home.

Mr Lywood said this was not a case of a gypsy who was on a piece of land without permission and should be evicted. 'By dint of his own hard work and labour he has bought his own land, got the family off the road, sent the children to school and integrated with local society. The council have not carried out their duties and are to blame for the fact that he is in this position. If there was a site for him to go to it would be different.'

Newland was fined £5. The prosecution said an application for accommodation would be considered sympathetically.

103

He being dead yet speaketh

*I*n 1995 I finally retired as leader of Goudhurst church. Since then gypsy churches have been springing up around Kent, there are about six pastors in Kent who are all gypsies by birth. Someone in France has a similar ministry to mine with the gypsies, although I've never met him. My ministry has been apostolic, with the gift of prophecy, but my main gift has always been evangelistic.

My ministry didn't stop when I retired. When Jennifer Rees-Larcombe was very ill, at one point her family thought she was dying and asked me to pray for her. Somehow it seemed to me that there was a lack of faith that she would be healed.

So after I had laid hands on her, I went back on my own and that's when the Lord told me that He was going to heal her, not now, but later. And that's exactly what happened, when a young girl prayed for her a few years later.

The gypsies still come to see me when they're in trouble and need help and advice. I'm the one they turn to. In 2002 there was a terrible accident which killed two gypsy lads and many people came to me for prayer and comfort. And until very recently I managed to preach once a week.

Only days before the fuel shortage in 2000, I was due to give the Sunday sermon and couldn't understand why the Lord was telling me to take money to church, as I never do. I picked up my purse, the minibus collected me as usual, and as we approached a petrol station, I heard the Lord say, 'Pull in and fill up.' I told the driver to stop, but she hadn't brought any money.

'That's OK, the Lord told me to bring this,' I said, handing over my wallet. We filled up, and two days later the nation was in the grip of the fuel shortage, but the bus had enough petrol to continue its vital work, right through the crisis.

By 2001 I was still doing a few prison visits, I have one man who got seven years for over-charging. I've known him for a long time, but he won't get converted because his wife hates a man she thinks killed her son. She's worn black for years and the husband says he won't be a hypocrite and get converted until the hatred is out of him as well. I'm hoping to go and see his wife, because if she could stop hating, he would, and then he'd be converted.

The Lord told me my fruit would remain, and it's incredible that there are three generations of believers after the people I first got converted, their children and grandchildren. There must be thousands of them, all going on with the Lord, gypsies who say they'd never heard the Gospel and never would have heard it if I hadn't gone to them. There was no-one else preaching to them.

And at the end of my ministry, the Lord had a place at Cornford House all ready for me. I've been able to spend plenty of time here in prayer, it's a wonderful place and the staff are so good. I did have a word from the Lord to say the house won't be closed. There's never been a time when I haven't felt God's presence, I have always known He is with me, even when I've gone wrong.

We should keep a short account with God, and the biggest thing I've done here is acknowledging that the break-up of the marriage was my fault and not my wife's. The Bible says, 'Husbands love their wives,'[37] and I didn't do that properly. There it is.

I'm very frail now, but since my conversion, I've never been afraid of death. A very great friend of mine was a spitfire pilot who was shot down three times but came through the war and was very wealthy. When I got converted our ways parted, but I was invited to his funeral in 1999. I'd never met his wife who he married late in life, but she'd heard all about me from him.

When I heard of his death, I phoned Kim and said, 'Death is not the end, and all believers meet.' It's not in the Bible, but it's a phrase the Lord gave me years earlier when I wanted wisdom for an unbelieving people I was working with.

Kim said, 'You say that with great assurance, I wish I could be so sure.'

I'm not afraid of death, why should I be? We'll meet Elijah, it'll be wonderful!

I remember two Christian spinster sisters from Horsmonden who truly loved each other and lived together all their lives. They were both in their eighties and one morning I saw one sister walking along, and her face was absolutely radiant, like an angel's. I realised something wonderful must have happened to her.

She didn't say good morning, just, 'Isn't it marvellous, isn't it wonderful? The Lord has just taken my sister!'

I thought – that's a lesson to me from the Lord if ever I had one - that's victory! We're basically selfish when we grieve - what we should do is rejoice that the man or woman we love is with the Lord. The Bible tells us that whether we live, or whether we die, we live for ever with Jesus, so we can't lose!

And I'm more fortunate than most, because I've already had a sight of heaven, and of Jesus.

All the long time John had been speaking, my attention had been gripped, and I was unable to look away, or question. But I'd never heard anything like this personal testimony, and knew readers wouldn't have the benefit of seeing and hearing John in the flesh, experiencing his searing honesty, and self-effacement.

I asked him, 'I'm worried people won't believe this John,

the things you've told me seem incredible.'

'Unless you've got faith these experiences *are* unbelievable, it's almost as if I'm making them up because they're so wonderful. But Jesus told his disciples to heal the sick, cleanse the lepers and raise the dead,[38] so we shouldn't be surprised when it happens. You mustn't worry about the people who will read this book, just do what the Lord says and write it down. It's *not* unbelievable, it's the truth, and God will always bless the truth. There's no need to fear about offending people or being too much for them, put it all down, and don't leave anything out, nothing.'

The expression on John's face had changed, his focus had faded, and I could tell he was back with me again, back from the past.

'I think I've said everything the Lord wants me to say, I have a very strong feeling that He's saying, 'No more, that's enough.' So it's up to you now, I've given you all that the Lord wants me to.

When this book comes to fruition, my story will help and encourage others, that's the reason the Lord wants it written down. I just thank and praise Him for all the wonderful things He has done and is going to do. Amen.'

Author's note

When time got the better of us at our first meeting, I produced a cassette recorder and asked John to make tapes before my next visit. He'd never owned or operated a machine like this, and was very concerned that he wouldn't manage. But he must have mastered the player, because tapes began to arrive a while later. As soon as I sat down to transcribe them I was dumbfounded. Where John occasionally recounted an incident that he'd already described to me, his version on tape was identical, almost word for word perfect with the notes I had taken.

That was when I first realised he couldn't be making up, imagining, or embellishing fact, because there would have been inconsistencies.

I sat at my keyboard, hearing the Etonian accent, voice raised as if he were speaking to a crowd at a distance, (I guess he didn't trust the microphone), speaking words that matched those on my screen.

'Forgive me!' I whispered, 'For doubting him.'

Meeting John Lywood had an enormous impact on my life. He prayed for me regularly, and sent long letters of encouragement, written in his familiar capital script in blue biro. I knew how much it cost John to write at all, the Parkinson's making writing difficult and painful.

7 March 'Wait on the Lord and let him speak to you from His word and be willing to do whatever he asks of you. Then He will lift you up from the slough of despond and '*bring you up out of the horrible pit, set your feet upon the rock and put a new song in your mouth, even praise unto our God.*'[39]

27 March 'Yesterday's faith will not do for today, and today's faith will not do for tomorrow. We need His strength, leading and guidance fresh each day. Remember, God is a God of love, and '*All things work together for good to them that* *love God.*'[40] He is not the author of illness or pain, but sometimes permits it for His own purpose to teach us lessons we can learn no other way. Get down on your knees and lay everything before the Lord, keeping nothing back. With my constant prayers and love in the Lord, John.'

12 November 'Above all, do not give up. That is what the Devil wants. *'We shall reap if we faint not.*'[41] A long time ago, a man said to me, 'Do not give up the things you can believe in, for some of the things you can't.' And remember, God is continually working for your ultimate good.'

Although we'd always hoped this book would be published soon after our first meeting in 2000, it wasn't to be.

Now, in summer 2005, John is very seriously ill and extremely frail. His health and his joy are fading, and I know it can't be long before he hears Jesus' beautiful words, '*Well done thou good and faithful servant, thou hast been faithful over a few things, I will make thee ruler over many, enter thou into the joy of thy Lord.*' [42]

No-one deserves to hear those words more than Charles John Lywood, the man who gave up everything for love of his God.

Endnotes

All Bible references are taken from John Lywood's own King James version.

[1] Hebrews 11 v 4
[2] Matthew 7 v 6
[3] 1 Corinthians 15 v 29
[4] Acts 5 v 32
[5] Acts 5
[6] John 14 v 6
[7] John 21 v 22
[8] 1 Peter 2 v 24
[9] Ezekiel 3 v 5
[10] Matthew 25 v 40
[11] 1 Corinthians 1 v 28
[12] Philippians 4 v 6-7
[13] Philippians 4 v 19
[14] Mark 8 v 36
[15] Matthew 6 v 33
[16] Isaiah 65 v 24
[17] Hebrews 11 v 1
[18] Deuteronomy 2 v 3
[19] Isaiah 25 v 10-11
[20] Mark 16 v 15-16
[21] 2 Corinthians 8 v 24
[22] Matthew 23 v 9
[23] Matthew 7 v 13-14
[24] Matthew 10 v 34-35
[25] Matthew 18 v 19
[26] Matthew 10 v 8
[27] Ephesians 4 v 28
[28] Matthew 7 v 20
[29] John 1 v 50
[30] James 5 v 15-16
[31] Acts 8 v 39
[32] Revelation 3 v 19
[33] Hebrews 13 v 8
[34] 2 Kings 10 v 10

[35] Revelation 3 v 20
[36] Mark 4 v 39
[37] Ephesians 5 v 25
[38] Matthew 10 v 8
[39] Psalm 40 v 2-3
[40] Romans 8 v 28
[41] Galatians 6 v 9
[42] Matthew 25 v 21

Helen Wilkinson is the author of *Dying to Live*, *The Missing Peace*, *Chinks* and the acclaimed best-seller *Peter's Daughter*. She was born in 1962, educated in Warwick and at London University, and now lives in Shrewsbury with her husband and daughter.